T0113388

THE Broken Hearth

Also by William J. Bennett

Counting by Race *(coauthor)*

Our Children and Our Country

The De-Valuing of America

The Book of Virtues

The Index of Leading Cultural Indicators

The Children's Book of Virtues

The Moral Compass

Our Sacred Honor

The Children's Book of Heroes

Body Count *(coauthor)*

The Death of Outrage

The Children's Book of America

The Educated Child *(coauthor)*

The Children's Book of Faith

The Children's Treasury of Virtues

THE Broken Hearth

Reversing the
Moral Collapse
of the
American Family

William J. Bennett

BROADWAY BOOKS
New York

A hardcover edition of this book was originally published in 2001
by Doubleday, a division of Random House, Inc. It is here reprinted
by arrangement with Doubleday.

BROADWAY BOOKS and its logo, a letter B bisected on the diagonal,
are trademarks of Random House, Inc.

Visit our website at www.broadwaybooks.com

First Broadway Books trade paperback edition published 2003

Book design by Donna Sinisgalli

Article: "Marriage's True Ends" by editors (May 17, 1996)
Citation: © 1996 Commonweal Foundation, reprinted with permission.
For Subscriptions, call toll-free: 1-888-495-6755.

The Library of Congress has cataloged the Doubleday hardcover edition
as follows:
Bennett, William J. (William John), 1943–
The broken hearth: reversing the moral collapse of the American
family / William J. Bennett.—1st ed.
p.   cm.
Includes index.
1. Family—United States. 2. Marriage—United States. 3. United
States—Social conditions—1980– 4. United States—Moral conditions.
I. Title.
HQ536 .B44 2001
306.8'0973—dc21   2001028873

ISBN-13: 978-0-767-90513-8

145052501

Acknowledgments

In *the* course of writing this book I sought the guidance of quite a number of authors who have made a lifelong study of marriage and the family. Many of their books and articles are mentioned in the pages that follow, and I take this opportunity to thank them collectively. Whatever their particular expertise, and wherever they may situate themselves on the political spectrum, I have benefited immensely from their work.

Special gratitude is owed to those who took time out from busy lives to help me as I thought through the argument of this book and formulated its major ideas. By offering comments, criticisms, and suggestions, they have made it better than it would otherwise have been. In particular, I want to thank M. Craig Barnes, David Blankenhorn, Don Browning, John J. DiIulio, Jr., Pat Fagan, David Frum, Maggie Gallagher, Steve Hayner, Charles Murray, David Murray, David Popenoe, and Barbara Dafoe Whitehead.

From the first days of this book, I availed myself of the wisdom and talents of my longtime friend and colleague Pete Wehner. Jason Bertsch, Kevin Cherry, and John Cribb also provided many helpful thoughts, corrections, and suggestions, as did my first editor and old friend Neal Kozodoy. Noreen Burns kept the office running while I was buried in fourteenth-century histories.

As always, my agent, Bob Barnett, provided counsel and friendship. Adam Bellow, my editor at Doubleday, brought professional insight and his own deep understanding of the issues. He made it a better book.

My wife, Elayne, and our sons, John and Joseph, have never failed to keep me mindful of the joys—and the challenges—of marriage and family life. They are my support, my stay, and my reward. And no matter what I do, Elayne keeps the hearth: warm and secure. It is to my family, then, that I dedicate this book.

CONTENTS

Preface

Last year, retiring United States Senator Daniel Patrick Moynihan was asked to identify the biggest change he had seen in his forty-year political career. Moynihan, a public intellectual who has served presidents of both parties with distinction, responded: "The biggest change, in my judgment, is that the family structure has come apart all over the North Atlantic world." This momentous transformation, Moynihan added, had occurred in "an historical instant. Something that was not imaginable forty years ago has happened."

Indeed it has, and we are all very much the worse for it. Virtually every opinion poll shows that the American people are deeply worried about the state of the family. They have good reason to be worried—even, I would say, frightened. Compared to a generation ago, American families today are much less stable; marriage is far less central; divorce, out-of-wedlock births, and cohabitation are vastly more common; and children are more vulnerable and neglected, less well-off, and less valued. Public attitudes toward marriage, sexual ethics, and child-rearing have radically altered for the worse.

In sum, the family has suffered a blow that has no historical precedent—and one that has enormous ramifications for American society. To be sure, there are some among us who, for reasons of their own, have welcomed the family's dissolution; a number of them—and their arguments—will be duly making their appearance in the course of this book. On the other side, there are some who, having taken the full measure of social loss entailed in the "coming-apart" Senator Moynihan referred to, have succumbed to a near-fatalistic despair, concluding that we are so far sunk in decadence that nothing will pull us out of it.

One of my major purposes in the pages that follow is to refute and repudiate the "liberationists" among us. But in some ways that task, arduous as it is, is easier than dealing with the apathy and surrender of those who see no way out. And so another of my major purposes will be to show why such feelings of surrender are misplaced and even morally unworthy of us. Bad as is the situation of the American family, we still have within us the power to change our ways and reclaim our legacy.

But my first task is to place the dissolution of the American family in its proper context. What is the state of marriage and the family in the first decade of the twenty-first century? How extensive is the damage? What might account for it? Is it irreversible? These are the sorts of questions I explore and try to answer in Chapter One.

Understanding social change of such magnitude concerning matters that touch on the most delicate and intimate areas of human life is a very large challenge—the more so since the change has taken place in so compressed a period of time and is not yet over. There are things we simply do not now comprehend. But our inability to explain everything does not mean we cannot make sense of some things. For there are, in fact, many things we do know and many other things we can reasonably surmise through the exercise of common sense and with the aid of history and human experience.

Hence my second task, which is to place our current situation in a broader historical perspective. How have marriage and family evolved over the ages? This is the story narrated in Chapter Two. It has many twists and turns, and it will, I think, surprise and intrigue many readers. In looking at five distinct periods in the history of the Western world, we will find that the institution of marriage has been anything but static; to the contrary, it has frequently adapted to new circumstances and has often become stronger and better as a result. At the same time, there are certain essentials that have remained relatively constant—core purposes that we need to fight mightily to preserve and protect.

Next, I take up what I consider to be the most important contemporary challenges to marriage and the modern family: cohabitation, illegitimacy, fatherlessness, homosexual unions, and divorce. In the three chapters that deal with these topics, I explore the principal arguments made by those who either favor contemporary developments, or accept them as inevitable, or believe they represent viable alternatives to "traditional" arrangements. My attempt to respond to these arguments is, I hope, candid, civil, and intellectually serious.

But my point in these chapters, as throughout this book, is not to engage in debate merely for debate's sake. Rather, it is actively to counter the growing acceptance of certain ideas—the idea, for example, that all arrangements (single mother, single father, gay partners, two-parent families) are essentially equivalent when it comes to raising children. To put it another way, the point is to give public expression to the private concerns of many Americans, to reinforce moral sentiments they may still hold but are now hesitant to act on or even articulate, and to attempt to persuade those who do not share such concerns.

Ideas have consequences, Richard Weaver famously wrote, and bad ideas can have baleful consequences. It is fashionable these days to say and to believe that matters like divorce, illegitimacy, cohabitation, and single-parenting are "private" matters that are not the business of the wider community. To which I would respond: There are few matters of more profound *public* consequence than the condition of marriage and families. Most of our social pathologies—crime, imprisonment rates, welfare, educational underachievement, alcohol and drug abuse, suicide, depression, sexually transmitted diseases—are manifestations, direct and indirect, of the crack-up of the modern American family.

In tracing the etiology of these pathologies, *The Broken Hearth* is, as I already intimated above, critical of contemporary liberalism and various "liberation" movements. But it also assesses the temptations of modernity and probes why so many Americans of nonideological persuasions do not hold the institution of marriage in high repute. To say it simply: We could not have experienced the scale of marital breakdown we have witnessed since 1960 unless huge numbers of our fellow citizens—conservative and liberal, believers and nonbelievers alike—had willingly detached themselves from once-solemn commitments made to spouses and children.

Finally, this book attempts to articulate some of the forgotten purposes of marriage and family. Too often in this debate, it strikes me, even the advocates of the family speak of it the way a mother might speak of spinach to an unwilling child: You might not enjoy it, but it's good for you. This needs to be redressed. Commitment, hard work, and perseverance are indeed essential elements in making a modern family succeed, but, today no less than yesterday or the day before, the rewards are matchless, taking the form of love, deep friendship, tenderness, mutuality, the refinement of the soul—and much laughter to boot.

I am no Pollyanna, and I do not believe that every marriage that is entered into in good faith can, or must, last forever, no matter what. My own mother divorced when I was five, remarried several times, and held two jobs outside the home; I saw my father only on weekends, and the various stepfathers in my life ran the usual gamut from good to bad. I am, therefore, the last person to idealize or sentimentalize family life. Still, we need to reclaim the ideal itself, so that it may serve as a guidepost, something high and estimable that we strive to attain. One reason so many American families are dissolving, or never forming, is that many of us have forgotten *why* we believe—and why we *should* believe—in the family. In the pages that follow, I try to answer those questions as well.

Let me offer a few additional observations. Divorce, out-of-wedlock births, fatherlessness, cohabitation, and the gay rights agenda are phenomena that affect virtually the entire Western world—which means, among other things, that what is happening in the United States is not unique. The engine driving the crack-up of the American family is cross-cultural and entangled in modernity itself. For a variety of reasons, however, I confine myself largely to America. It is the nation I know best and love most and feel best equipped to comment on. That is not to say that what applies to America does not apply to other Western nations as well; it does.

This book rests on moral precepts most people agree about. It also reflects an understanding of marriage and family life rooted in traditional Christian and Jewish teachings, and, more specifically, in my Catholic faith. One certainly does not have to hold to these faiths to agree with the arguments I propound; there are a raft of nonreligious reasons to support marriage and the family. But the effort to pry discussions of these matters away from the religious context altogether is, I believe, both wrong and counterproductive. The Christian and Jewish understanding of family is no myth. Not only does it reflect deep human truths, it contributes a vital perspective that mere social science is powerless to provide.

I fully recognize that in arguing for many of the positions I do, I will be accused of wanting to "turn back the clock." That happens not to be true. While I believe that we desperately need to recover much of what has been lost, I explicitly say that certain trends are irreversible, and, at least in some cases, thankfully so, for there are things in the past that are worth leaving behind—including the unequal status accorded to women for much of Western history. The notion that "conservatives" believe otherwise is a disingenuous fiction.

In fact, the whole turning-back-the-clock argument is itself often disingenuous, meant more as a conversation stopper than as a serious point, and designed to make those who hold traditional views appear antediluvian. C. S. Lewis had a wonderful rejoinder to this ploy:

> I would rather get away from that whole idea of clocks. We all want progress. But progress means getting nearer to the place where you want to be. And if you have taken a wrong turning, then to go forward does not get you any nearer. If you are on the wrong road, progress means doing an about-turn and walking back to the right road; and in that case the man who turns back soonest is the most progressive . . . [and] going back is the quickest way on.

If we are to get nearer to the place we want to be, we will have to correct some big mistakes and revisit some disastrously wrong turns. This will require much of us, both personally and as citizens. Although there is simply no substitute for the daily love and devotion of individual husbands and wives and parents, there is also a vital need to affirm publicly, and to defend publicly, the institution that is the keystone in the arch of civilization—a keystone in desperate need of repair.

This is my third decade in public life. I have served two presidents and written on subjects ranging from crime, education, and welfare to race, immigration, popular culture, and much else. But the enervation of both marriage and family life is, to me, the most perilous development of modern times. To help fortify them is the reason I wrote this book.

The State of Marriage and the Family

I

For years, the rock star Melissa Etheridge and her partner, the film-maker Julie Cypher, had been asked to name the biological father of their two little children, Bailey and Beckett. Tired of keeping it a mystery, Etheridge and Cypher (who had left her husband in order to live with Etheridge and who then bore the two children) revealed their secret in the February 3, 2000, issue of *Rolling Stone*: The father was the fifty-eight-year-old rock legend David Crosby.

As Etheridge and Cypher explained, several years ago, while vacationing in Hawaii, they had dropped in to visit Crosby and his wife, Jan. During the conversation, Etheridge and Cypher mentioned their wish to have a child. Jan Crosby volunteered, "What about David?" Crosby, who concedes that he did not know the couple well, immediately agreed. "I don't even think it should be a big deal," he said later.

In the magazine interview, Etheridge said, "I know that because of the procreation of our species, that it was man and woman, and that's the way it was all built. But two loving parents—that's all a kid needs. Two men, two women, a man and a woman, whatever." In a subsequent television interview she added: "I do not believe that my children will be wanting in any way because they didn't have a father in the home every single day. What they have in the home is two loving parents. I think that puts them ahead of the game." Be sides, interjected Cypher, "The definition of family is changing and evolving in our society so quickly."

Crosby, who has not assumed any parental duties toward the two children, agrees: "Maybe it's a good thing for a lot of straight families to see that this is not something strange. . . . If, you know, in due time, at a distance, [Bailey and Beckett] are proud of who their genetic dad is, that's great."

At the end of the *Rolling Stone* interview, Cypher went to retrieve a photo album. "Look at this," she said, producing a photograph of a smiling group of people, including the two youngsters. "There's David, his son, his other son, his daughter-in-law . . . his granddaughter . . . his daughter."

"And there's my mother," added Etheridge.

On the back of the photograph, Cypher had written an inscription: "Twenty-first-century family."

Melissa Etheridge and Julie Cypher, embodiments of twenty-first-century ideas in more ways than one, and role models for countless young Americans, have since broken up.

Two years ago, the British press reported on events surrounding the birth of twin girls, Danielle and Emma. The story began with the desire of a wealthy Italian businessman and his Portuguese wife, living in France, to have a third child. (They were already parents, via surrogate births, of a son and a daughter.) The couple asked Claire Austin, an English surrogate mother, to bear the baby for them, and then went looking for donors of sperm and eggs. The latter came from an anonymous Englishwoman, the former from an American man. On February 28, 1999, a doctor in Athens carried out the procedure of implantation.

Twenty weeks into the pregnancy, Miss Austin learned she was carrying twin girls. Her doctor was appalled: The couple wanted a boy—one boy. Miss Austin was told she should terminate the pregnancy. She was unwilling to do so, but she had no formal agreement to appeal to (surrogacy is illegal in France). Nor did she know to whom the children belonged—after all, they were genetically related neither to her nor to either member of the commissioning couple. Eventually she found Growing Generations, an adoption agency based in Los Angeles that specialized in "unconventional parents." The agency located a couple living in Hollywood: Tracey Stern, a scriptwriter for the television programs *ER* and *Buffy the Vampire Slayer*, and Julia Salazar. Stern and Salazar agreed to adopt the twins, who are now being looked after—by a nanny from Puerto Rico.

What anecdotes suggest, research confirms: Over the last four decades, marriage and family life have undergone an extraordinary transformation, yielding arrangements as temporary and as fragile—and as widespread—as those detailed above. "The scale of marital breakdown in the West since 1960 has no historical precedent and seems unique," exclaims the distinguished historian Lawrence Stone. "At no time in history, with the possible exception of Imperial Rome, has the institution of marriage been more problematic than it is today," adds the demographer Kingsley Davis. In the judgment of James Q. Wilson, America's preeminent social scientist, we are witnessing a "profound, worldwide, long-term change in the family that is likely to continue for a long time."

Scholars now speak of an ongoing trend toward a "postmarriage" society, one in which commitments to spouses and children are increasingly limited, contingent, and easily broken. Marriage itself is far less permanent, and far less of a social norm, than ever before in living memory. Concomitantly, Americans have seen a stunning rise in (among other social indices) divorce, out-of-wedlock births, unwed teen mothers, abortion, the numbers of children living in single-parent homes, and the numbers of cohabiting couples. In many of these categories, our country now has the dubious honor of leading the industrialized world.

A little later on, I will be tracing the devastating effect of these trends on all sectors of our society, and especially on the poor and the defenseless among us. But I should note right at the outset that not everybody agrees the effects *have* been devastating; that, to my mind, is part of the problem. A few years ago, for example, Shere Hite, the author-researcher of the Hite Reports on human sexuality, urged upon us "that the breakdown of the family is a *good* thing" (emphasis added) and that today's "new living arrangements" may be "one of the most important turning points of the West." Last year, *Time* magazine published an article by the influential feminist Barbara Ehrenreich on the desirability of institutionalizing the crack-up of the family by formally replacing yesterday's "one-size-fits-all model of marriage" with a different and better model: "renewable marriages, which get re-evaluated every five to seven years, after which they can be revised, recelebrated, or dissolved with no, or at least fewer, hard feelings."

These voices are not alone; we shall be hearing from others like them in the course of this chapter. What they suggest is that when it comes to marriage and family life, everything is now up for grabs. More so than at any other time in human history, we share no common understanding of marriage and the family. Marriage itself, detached from any objective foundation, is seen by many as possessing little or no intrinsic worth but as being a means to an end: the end, that is, of "personal happiness" or "fulfillment." In the quest for fulfillment, spouses and children are often looked upon not as persons to be loved and valued for their own sake but as objects to be acquired, enjoyed, and discarded.

Like the breakdown of the family itself, this cultural deconstruction of family life and its purposes has no historical precedent. It has left us open to doubts about some of our most basic understandings: about the parent-child bond, about marital permanence, about the link between marriage, sex, and procreation. It has already dragged innumerable children and adults into the very opposite of "personal happiness," and it threatens to undo altogether a precious historical achievement.

II

It is the core argument of this book that the nuclear family, defined as a monogamous married couple living with their children, is vital to civilization's success. We may build cities of gold and silver, but if the family fails, fewer and fewer of our children will ever learn to walk in justice and virtue. Why I believe this to be so will become clearer as we go along. But even those who welcome it cannot dispute that the nuclear family is indeed failing.

Let me count a few of the ways.

Divorce: A generation ago, the odds were one in four that a child would witness his parents' breakup; today, they are one in two. Since 1960, a forty-year period in which the marriage rate has declined by a third, the divorce rate (despite small recent improvements) has more than doubled.

The year 1974 was a landmark of sorts. In that year, divorce replaced death as the principal cause of family dissolution. Today, so deeply entrenched is divorce that Lawrence Stone has called it as much a part of our culture and our lives as death and taxes.

Out-of-Wedlock Births: In 1994, for the first time in American history, more than *half* of all firstborn children were conceived or born out of wedlock—the culmination of a long-term trend. Among teenagers, that trend is even more alarming; today, over three-quarters of all births to teenagers occur outside of marriage, while in fifteen of our nation's largest cities, the teenage out-of-wedlock birth ratio exceeds ninety percent.

Single-Parent Families: Between 1960 and 1998, the percentage of single-parent families—overwhelmingly headed by mothers—more than tripled. It is estimated that more than one-third of American children are now living apart from their biological fathers, and about forty percent of such children have not seen their fathers in at least a year.

Cohabitation: Between 1960 and 2000, the number of couples cohabiting increased more than elevenfold, from under five hundred thousand to five and a half million, with the biggest spike occurring in the 1990s. Today, more than half of all marriages are preceded by a period of cohabitation, and the number is even higher among men and women in their twenties and thirties, for whom cohabitation is *replacing* marriage.

That these arrangements are inherently unstable has been amply confirmed by research: According to the sociologist Pamela J. Smock, "only about one-sixth of cohabitations last at least three years and only one-tenth last five years or more." As for couples who cohabit before marriage, contrary to popular wisdom, the chances of a subsequent divorce are almost *double* those for couples who marry without prior cohabitation. What all this means for the many children born to cohabiting couples is depressingly plain.

Fertility: The fertility rate, which peaked at 3.65 children per woman at the height of the baby boom in 1957, declined rapidly and has settled at around 2.0 today. It is true that with the one big exception of the post—World War II period, fertility has been on the decline for several centuries—but since 1975, for the first time in our history, we have been hovering right at or below the rate necessary to replace the population, and are likely to remain there. From being a child- and family-oriented society, we are becoming a society in which children are not only less heard but less seen.

The results of the 2000 Census, released in May 2001, confirmed these trends. The number of Americans living alone, *The New York Times* reported, surpassed the number of married couples with children. During the 1990s, the number of families headed by single mothers grew at a rate nearly five times that of families headed by a mother and father. The Census counted 5.5 million unmarried couples, up from 3.2 million in 1990. As *The Washington Post* summarized, "The statistics showed no reversal of a decades-long national trend away from the historically dominant household, married couples with children."

Statistics are cold things—in this case, properly so. For the picture conjured up by these, and other statistics I could have cited just as readily, is a chilling one: Since 1960, fewer people are marrying, they are doing so later in life, they are having fewer children, they are spending less time with the children they do have, and they are divorcing much more frequently. Those who do not marry are having sexual relations at an earlier age and contracting sexually transmitted diseases at much higher rates, cohabiting in unprecedented numbers, and having a record number of children out of wedlock. Finally, more children than ever before live with only one parent.

These trends have been truly and deeply harmful to us as individuals and to us as a society. So I believe, and so I intend to demonstrate in greater detail in the middle chapters of this book. There is, of course, still no dearth of influential voices celebrating the crack-up of the "repressive" nuclear family, or arguing that the massive changes we have experienced are merely adjustments to the form of family life and not a fundamental threat to the institution itself. Editorializing about the 2000 Census figures I cited above, *The New York Times* instructed readers that "the nuclear family itself, especially in its suburban, Ozzie and Harriet form, is a reduction of what family has meant in most places at most times," and that "the nuclear family is not the only kind of family or even the only healthy kind of family." Even President George W. Bush's domestic policy adviser, Margaret LaMontagne, when asked on television about the figures showing the decline of the modern nuclear family, shrugged them off with a "So what?"

But the case for indifference, insofar as it is based on facts and not mere emotion, is getting weaker by the day. Research (as well as common sense) tells us that in the vast majority of cases, children are better off—physically, emotionally, psychologically, educationally, and financially—when they are raised in intact, two-parent families. In the confirming words of Sara McLanahan and Gary Sandefur, the authors of *Growing Up with a Single Parent*: "If we were asked to design a system for making sure that children's basic needs were met, we would probably come up with something quite similar to the two-parent family ideal."

Other scholars, too, have come to this conclusion, in some cases reluctantly and after years of denying that the family was an institution in trouble. The social analyst Mary Jo Bane, who once dismissed marital decline as "more myth than fact," later came to acknowledge that "the change [in the American family] is astonishing both for its size and for the speed with which it has happened." In the early 1980s, the economist Sar A. Levitan coauthored the book *What's Happening to the American Family?*, whose point of view was that "currently fashionable gloom-and-doom scenarios miss the essential process of adjustment and change." But already in the book's second edition, less than a decade later, Levitan and his colleagues were expressing alarm: "Widespread family breakdown is bound to have a pervasive and debilitating impact not only on the quality of life but on the vitality of the body politic as well."

I myself would put those last, carefully understated words in italics, thus: *"Widespread family breakdown is bound to have a pervasive and debilitating impact not only on the quality of life but on the vitality of the body politic."* And I would, if I could, inscribe them on the heart of every policymaker, every parent, and every prospective parent in the land.

III

But what exactly accounts for the fracturing of the American family and the weakening of our commitment to marriage? What has led us to this perilous moment?

Explaining social change is at best an imperfect science: We do better at grasping what happened than at understanding why it happened. If this is so in the case of discrete events, it is triply so in the case of something as large and complicated as family life. What we can state with confidence is that the transformations in American family life since 1960 cannot be reduced to any single cause. They are, rather, the result of a confluence of factors, some of them material, others, for want of a better word, cultural. As to which of them is cause and which is effect, such is the seamless nature of life in society that it is often impossible to say.

Some of these factors are fundamental shifts in moral attitudes and the rise of a radical individualistic ethos; the advent of the sexual revolution, the pill, and legalized abortion; new rules governing male-female relations and expectations of family life; the increased participation of women in the workforce; a fierce assault directed *against* marriage and the family; the dramatic reshaping of family law; the pervasive influence of popular culture; affluence and the rise of a consumerist mentality.

Let me begin our discussion with one of the most important of these "root causes," the massive shift in cultural, personal, and sexual values that began in the mid to late 1960s and took hold in the 1970s.

In those years, the years of the New Left and the counterculture, of campus rioting and the spread of recreational drugs, Americans came to place a much higher premium on individualism, on unrestricted personal liberty, and on personal choice. Authority and traditional institutions were called into question. It became unfashionable to enter judgments on a whole range of behaviors and attitudes. We *de*valued concepts like personal responsibility and self-denial, and we *re*valued the impulses of self-fulfillment and self-actualization. The self, in Allan Bloom's withering phrase, became our "modern substitute for the soul."

This development was evident to almost everyone who lived through that era, and to this day its signs are everywhere around us—in books, magazines, songs, movies, campus life, daily conversation, and, inevitably, in our conventional views of marriage and the family.

We know, for example, that during the past four decades and until just recently, the percentage of Americans who believe that "the family should stay together for the sake of the children" sharply declined. We know that Americans today are simultaneously more concerned with achieving professional and financial success and less willing to invest time, money, and energy in family life. And we know that an increasing number of people believe that divorce, adultery, out-of-wedlock birth, cohabiting before marriage, and the like are strictly "personal" and no business of the wider community.

How is it that within the space of a few decades, the individualist ethic should have spawned a new and greater public tolerance of behaviors once deemed problematic, if not altogether beyond the pale? A key role, certainly, was played by another of the factors I named earlier: the widespread availability of contraceptives on the one hand and legalized abortion on the other. Men and women today can have sex more promiscuously, more casually, and with much lower odds of pregnancy and childbirth. For the first time, on a large scale, sex has been de-linked from both marriage and procreation.

The results of this revolutionary shift are all around us, in our homes, on our streets, in the books we read and the movies and television shows we watch. Sexual promiscuity, heterosexual and homosexual alike, is a fact of life, incorporated into the mentality and often the behavior of even the youngest adolescents, and reinforced even by well-meaning adults through programs like the free distribution of condoms in schools. As for the by-products of increased promiscuity, the more measurable ones can be found in high rates of abortion *and* out-of-wedlock births, as well as the relentless march of sexual diseases both old and new.* Whatever one's view of the benefits that have accrued from the sexual revolution, there is no denying that in its wake we as a society have had to pay dearly, and we go on paying every day.

Indeed, as is often the case with revolutions, the ones who have ended up paying the highest price for our regime of sexual freedom are its supposed beneficiaries. The pill and the sexual revolution were hailed as great liberators of women. Instead, as George Akerlof

* Despite recent, small reductions in the abortion rate, more than twenty-five percent of pregnancies still end in abortion.

of the University of California has argued, the "reproductive technology shock" experienced by the United States in the 1970s had the
effect of "immiserating" women—especially, but not exclusively,
women who wished to avoid premarital sex.

Prior to that time, sexual relations were conditioned on a promise of marriage if pregnancy resulted. hence the phenomenon of the
"shotgun wedding." Now, what came increasingly to be expected in
premarital relationships was sexual activity without commitment,
putting special pressure on women who wanted children or who did
not want an abortion for moral or religious reasons—the pressure,
that is, of losing their partners if they refused sex. This may help
explain why, contrary to every expectation, the widespread availability of both contraception and abortion was accompanied by such a
huge increase in out-of-wedlock births.

Akerlof and his colleague Linda Yellin also point out that before
the sexual revolution, men were expected to assume responsibility
for the women with whom they had sexual relations. But as pregnancy and childbirth increasingly became the choice of the woman
alone, men felt less duty bound either to marry or to provide for the
welfare of the child. Sex became commitment free. Men, liberated
from the consequence of their acts, drew further and further away
from lasting attachment to family life.

IV

At one time, wearing a wedding band meant you were off limits. Today that is less and less the case. In recent decades we have seen the
rise of a phenomenon characterized (by Arizona State University
Professor Bernard Farber) as "permanent availability." More and
more people—married people—want to remain on the marriage
market, where what is on offer can look like a vast improvement

over what they already have. Couples know each other's flaws and shortcomings all too well; when we see people in settings where they are at their best (in dress, manner, and style), the impression can be undeniably alluring.

This brings me to still another of the factors on my list. Pastoral counselors tell me of a recurring problem they confront: extremely high, unreasonably high, expectations surrounding marriage and family life. No doubt because of the premium we place on the idea of personal happiness, many of us invest hopes in our spouses and families that can never be realized, expecting them to meet all our needs. As a result, many become frustrated and disillusioned and give up on family life entirely, never allowing it to become what it *can* be: a sanctuary; a setting of intimacy, companionship, and deep friendship; a place where people learn patience, grace, and the joy of giving oneself fully.

Demanding more, we obligate ourselves less. M. Craig Barnes, pastor of the National Presbyterian Church, invokes an apt biblical allusion to express this syndrome of our time: "As Adam and Eve discovered, it is in reaching for more than we were created to have that we lose the really good garden we were given. And then we realize it was paradise. But paradise lost."

A related point: In the past, the happiness and satisfaction attained through marriage and family life depended to a large extent on the tangible, practical benefits that also accrued from them—including economic security, social standing, and the performance of complementary domestic duties. In reciprocal fashion, these very things tended to be enhanced by marital stability. Today, however, marriage is based much more on certain intangible, subjective benefits, including feelings of love, emotional fulfillment, and physical attractiveness. These are wonderful qualities to look for in a marriage; but they are also much less stable criteria, less reliable, more subject to inconstancy.

In Robert Bellah's *Habits of the Heart,* a 1985 book based on a massive five-year study of American communities, any number of people—wives and husbands, corporate managers, psychotherapists, businessmen, civic activists—reported how hard it was to commit themselves to another person, believing, as many of them did, that "in the end you're really alone." Where does such a belief come from? In the past, husbands and wives had well-defined roles. Today, thanks to the sexual and social revolution of our time, definitions blur, and disappointed hopes can turn rapidly into hopes abandoned.

"My generation was the first to confront equality of the sexes," says Steven L. Nock, a fifty-year-old researcher at the University of Virginia. "As a result, many reacted to the changed rules by fleeing from marriage. I suspect that our children, who've grown up with gender equality as a given, will be less likely to flee marriage." For the sake of those children, and even more so for the sake of *their* children, we can only hope Professor Nock is right. But it will not happen on its own. As the road out and away was swift and easy, the road back will be long and difficult.

V

Changed expectations are only part of the story. Another part has to do with the withering, sustained *attack* on marriage and the nuclear family that was mounted during the late 1960s and early 1970s. Whenever conservatives raise this topic, they open themselves to ridicule as reactionaries. By contrast, one senses among many liberals a deep ideological investment in the liberationist movement of the 1960s and 1970s, which inhibits them from plainly acknowledging that movement's costs. But the fact is that out of that era there really did emerge some pernicious, and debilitating, attitudes, many of them by now deeply entrenched in our mores and culture.

In 1977, the social historian Christopher Lasch—no conservative, he—wrote *Haven in a Heartless World: The Family Besieged.* Lasch's book chronicles the course of the sexual revolution, the counterculture, feminism, the celebration of "alternate lifestyles," "creative divorce," and "open marriage." In those years, feminists and others routinely accused marriage and the nuclear family of promoting neurosis. Children were said to be helpless "prisoners" over whom parents enjoyed "nearly absolute power." Because parenthood was held to be too important to be left to amateurs, arguments were advanced for "professionalizing" child care by assigning children to special clinics, to couples specially trained and certified for parenthood, or to communes.

Three decades ago, it was also said that the future of marriage depended on "kicking the togetherness habit." Husbands and wives needed to respect each other's need for individuality, "self-awareness," and "personal growth." According to experts, the key was to "get in touch" with your own feelings by rejecting such rigidly defined social roles as "husband" and "wife," "father" and "mother." A revealing phrase at the time, used by authors Nena and George O'Neill (authors of the best-selling 1972 book *Open Marriage: A New Life Style for Couples*) was "nonbinding commitments"—an oxymoronic phrase invoked, as Lasch pointed out, without any sense of irony.

Still another influential book that appeared in the 1970s was *The Future of Marriage* by the distinguished scholar Jessie Bernard. While Bernard did not, like her more radical colleagues, predict the end of marriage, she argued for a "future of options" and "new forms of relationships": communes and polygamy, trial marriages, group marriages, weekend marriages, nonsexual marriages, marital "swinging," cohabitation, limited-commitment marriages. About the consequences of all this she was thoroughly untroubled; in prin-

ciple, wrote Bernard, there was "nothing in human nature that favored one kind of marriage over any other."

Today, in recalling some of the wilder words of the radicals of
the late '60s and early '70s, one is almost tempted to laugh: at their
trendiness and faddishness, their naiveté and foolishness, their false
hopes and sloppy rhetoric. One also recalls that the roots of this sort
of heedless experimentalism go deep in our national history.
Nathaniel Hawthorne's wonderfully acerbic novel, *The Blithedale
Romance* (1852), skewers one such early experiment in communal
utopianism, Brook Farm in Massachusetts. But the difference is that
in the 1960s and '70s, and for the first time, truly significant numbers of Americans took the liberationist critique of society seriously
and, cheered on by intellectuals and social scientists, acted upon it.

To be sure, "significant numbers" hardly means everybody.
Wife-swapping and "open marriage" did not become the rage of
American life. But there can be no question that the radicalizing talk
had an effect, fracturing the lens through which many people
viewed commitment, marriage, or parental authority. While Americans did not give up on the family or jettison all of its traditions,
much changed. Revolutions, even revolutions that do not fully succeed, leave the landscape permanently altered.

For those who unleashed the philosophical wrecking ball against
marriage and the nuclear family, the aim was clear. Their mission
was to shatter an oppressive and sexist institution, in the certainty
that out of the ruins would emerge all sorts of wonderful things. But
it was not to be. By the late 1970s and early 1980s, the returns (em-
pirical and otherwise) were coming in. We have already reviewed
some of them: those extraordinary leaps in divorce and abandonment, out-of-wedlock births, abortions, cohabitation, and sexual
promiscuity. Also well documented by the 1980s were a growing unhappiness in marriage, more sexual hang-ups, more child neglect

and abuse, and less trust and more friction between men and women. Like binge drinkers, Americans, in the words of Daniel Yankelovich, had "learned a great deal from their bruising encounter with new self-expressive values."

It turned out, in short, that there *was* a high price to pay—a price in social carnage and wrecked lives—for so cavalierly trying to overturn our most important institution. Many Americans now seem to know this: A January 2001 poll by Gallup showed a significant number citing ethics, morals, and family decline as the most serious problem facing the nation; a somewhat earlier poll by Hart-Teeter showed a plurality concerned above all with "the breakdown of the family." While they may not wish to return to what they believe was a rigid and constricting past, or to give up the extraordinary gains they have made in personal freedom, many of today's Americans do wish for greater social cohesion, stability, and family bonds.

This is a tough balancing act, however, and it forces us to decide among competing values. One thing we know for sure is that we cannot, by snapping our fingers, simply cause strong marriages and a healthy family life to come into being. We will need to reform attitudes and habits, laws and social arrangements, that have by now become ingrained.

VI

One such arrangement has to do with work. In a period of a few decades, America has gone from a society in which most married women were full-time homemakers to one in which both spouses frequently work outside the home. Just to get a feel for the scope of the change, the proportion of married women in the labor force who have children under six years of age jumped from under twenty percent in 1960 to over sixty percent in 1996.

The increased participation by women in the paid labor force has been good in some important respects: Barriers have been broken down, and ancient prejudices have receded. Women who want to enter the workforce find far more acceptance and freedom, and greater professional and personal satisfaction, than was once the case. And working women have obviously made tremendous contributions to the economy and to society. But these trends have also had enormous repercussions on male-female relationships, marriage, and children, and advancement in some areas has come at the expense of regression in others.

One of the legacies of the social revolution of our time has been to stigmatize stay-at-home mothers as antiquated and unfulfilled. Particularly in the 1970s and 1980s, such mothers were made to feel as if they had to apologize for the lives they had chosen—for, in effect, siding with their children instead of with the cause of women's liberation. In a 1975 discussion, the famous French feminist Simone de Beauvoir went so far as to assert that "no woman should be authorized to stay at home to raise her children. . . . Women should not have that choice, precisely because if there is such a choice, too many women will make that one."

Yet for many women the greatest satisfaction in life is to be found in devoting themselves to the upbringing of their children. Many women do not *want* to enter the labor force: For them, the prospect of missing out on the everyday joys and trials of motherhood—the first steps, the first words, trips to the store, time spent at the playground or in playgroups, the chance to offer comfort in response to tears of frustration or fear—is unthinkable.

Mothers who forgo a career altogether, or who put their career on hold for a time in order to stay home and care for their young children, are worthy of praise. Many of them are making a costly personal sacrifice: In emotional and even in physical terms, it often would be less demanding, and more lucrative, to join the labor force.

An obvious subset of this discussion is the issue of day care. This is a subject about which feelings run extraordinarily high, especially among professional women: a tribute, perhaps, to the very ambivalence many of them feel in trying to reconcile their longing to achieve with their concerns about the effects of their absence from home on their children. And because day care *is* about children—about the next generation—the debate about it tends, for many of us, to pull into its orbit every other problem and every other nagging discontent with the often ramshackle structure of our family lives.

My own view—to state it right from the start—is that day care is no substitute for a parent's unqualified love and devotion, patience, empathy, and unhurried attention. The writer Karl Zinsmeister puts it this way, and I agree: "A child and a parent are bound eternally, by blood and destiny. A day-care worker is doing a job." Of course, not every child comes from a caring and loving home; and of course, the quality of day care varies considerably. But in the large majority of cases, day care cannot measure up to the devotion of a mother, and we are embracing shadow and myth if we think otherwise.

I fully recognize that for some women, staying home full-time to raise young children can be a miserable experience; they feel overwhelmed and isolated, their interests seem to narrow, and they may receive little encouragement or assistance from their husbands. Pressuring such a woman to stay home, or making her feel guilty for working outside, can cause resentments that may eventually manifest themselves in her relationship with her child. It is worth pointing out as well that many employed mothers would dearly prefer to cut back or simply stay at home full-time, but go to work because they must.

Depending on circumstances, all sorts of compromises suggest themselves. One might be to work part-time; or to work out of one's home; or to coordinate a schedule that will allow a child to see his father or mother during part of the day; or to choose personal forms of child care (like grandparents or nannies) in lieu of institutional care; or to sacrifice other things in life in order to spend as many nonwork hours with children as possible. One emerging trend is for mothers to stay at home while their children are very young and then reenter the labor force once they enroll in school. But whatever the course chosen, conflicts are inevitable.

How could it be otherwise? A truth that has been obscured in recent years is that once a man and a woman decide to have a child, the well-being of that child has chief claim over virtually everything else—including, surely, career ambitions and all-consuming jobs. But having both mothers and fathers in the workforce means that *both* parents spend less time with their offspring: a combined average of seventeen hours per week according to a University of Maryland study, as compared with thirty hours in 1965.

Overwork and lack of time spent with children are prevalent enough to merit their own term in the social science lexicon: the "parenting deficit." This deficit is something that, no doubt, more men than women need to take to heart and to act upon. It is a fact that *fatherlessness*, not women in the workforce, is a far more serious problem when it comes to the absence of parental time with children, and that is a subject I will address in due course. But even in two-parent families, in the nature of things the brunt of the burden will continue to fall upon women.

The bottom line is this: The increased participation of wives and mothers in the workforce is, for many, a decidedly mixed blessing. On the one hand, women have become less economically dependent on men; in, for example, a situation where a husband emotionally or physically abuses his wife, she may now be able to leave without necessarily fearing that destitution awaits her or her children. On the other hand, there can be little doubt that the kind of casual divorce we see today—in which people just drift apart and then call it quits, or leave for reasons of boredom or "self-discovery"—is itself trace-able in some measure to the fact that women can more readily exit marriage than was once the case. To which some scholars add that a wife's economic independence also makes it easier for a husband to abandon *her* if and when he so chooses.

The ease with which marriages dissolve and families break up today also creates palpable insecurity among many husbands and wives. With abandonment and divorce so deeply woven into our cul-tural fabric, how many are really confident of a lifelong marriage? This lack of confidence can make wives reluctant to leave the labor market even if they want to. After all, they may be only a divorce away from having to return someday.

VII

There are certain things about which a society feels so strongly that they became codified in law. Both reflecting and helping to shape public sentiment, the law is, in the memorable words of Justice Holmes, "the witness and external deposit of our moral life." But what happens when our moral life changes?

For much of its history, America's legal system viewed marriage and the family as institutions deserving of support, protection, and a privileged status. According to the scholar Lenore J. Weitzman, "American divorce law, with historical roots in the English common law, was based on the underlying premise that marriage was a per-manent and cherished union which the Church—and then the state—had to protect and preserve."

But that legal outlook itself began to change, and radically so, in the latter half of the twentieth century. Harvard's Mary Ann Glen-don, perhaps the nation's foremost authority on the subject, has writ-ten that the late 1960s ushered in the most fundamental shift in family law since the Protestant Reformation. Until that point, marriage was considered to be a lifetime union (except in very rare instances), dedicated to procreation and child-rearing, sexually exclusive, and socially important. The domestic relations laws of the various states were organized around a "marriage-centered conception of the family."

No longer. The underlying assumption that divorce, for example, should be obtainable only for cause (e.g., adultery and desertion) has been essentially thrown out. Most marriages can now be dissolved by one spouse over the objections of the other, and without cause. The old system of alimony and property awards (based on the presumption that a husband has a duty to support his ex-wife financially) has been replaced by a system that assumes the "innocent" spouse in a divorce case should be self-sufficient and awards, if they are made, temporary. Family members can now sue one another, children born outside of marriage have the same legal rights as those born in marriage, and "the legal differences between formal and informal marriage have been blurred."

Above all, marriage is now viewed not as a covenant but simply as a *contract*, based on self-interest, convenience, and individual self-fulfillment. As contracts go, moreover, it is among the weakest in contemporary American society; in the words of the family scholar Maggie Gallagher, "We now live in a society where it is legally easier and less risky to dump a wife than to fire an employee."

Listen to the penetrating summary of Mary Ann Glendon:

The American story about marriage, as told in the law and in much popular literature, goes something like this: marriage is a relationship that exists primarily for the fulfillment of the individual spouses. If it ceases to perform this function, no one is to blame and either spouse may terminate it at will. After divorce, each spouse is expected to be self-sufficient. . . . *Children hardly appear in the story; at most they are rather shadowy characters in the background.* Other stories, of course, are still vigorous in American culture—about marriage as a union for life, for better or worse, even in sickness or poverty; stories about taking on responsibilities and carrying through; and about parenthood as an awesome commitment. But, by and large, they are not the ones that have been incorporated into the law. [emphasis added]

Three things should be noted in connection with this quotation. First, as with the issue of work, there is no denying that many women have benefited from the changes in marriage law, especially those women trapped in abusive or terminally miserable marriages. Second, America is not alone in this radical transformation of family law; almost every Western nation has done the same—although American law has "taken the idea of individual freedom to terminate a marriage" farther than any other. And third, some changes in family law predate the 1960s. But nothing compares with how, over the last three and a half decades, the courts have relentlessly drained the family of its institutional authority and given primacy to personal autonomy and individual liberties.

If you happen to believe that the traditional family is intrinsically oppressive of women and children, and if you happen to believe that the goal of law ought to be to liberate them from "the shackles of such intermediate groups as [the] family" (in the words of Harvard law professor Laurence Tribe), then these developments represent a great emancipation. But if you believe, as I do, that the nuclear family, while flawed and imperfect, remains the best institution ever devised for educating, nurturing, and protecting children and for assuring deep intimacy, commitment, and mutual support between a man and a woman, then these developments are surely among the most harmful of modern times.

VIII

I am certain—though I cannot prove it empirically—that the mass media have also exercised a cumulatively damaging impact on marriage and family ties. Others would put it more strongly and much more broadly: To them, so pernicious—so diabolical—have the mass media become, especially television and the movies, that they need to be firmly regulated, prevented from spewing their indecent images, their violence, and their lewd conversation into our living rooms and consciousness. Meanwhile, to still other Americans, any such talk raises the dread specter of censorship, of tampering with our precious First Amendment freedoms. Before attempting to adjudicate this dispute, let me postulate a few facts that I think no one would seriously deny.

The media possess extraordinary power to alter attitudes and moral sensibilities. They accomplish this both by sheer saturation—who among us can hope to escape their reach?—and through the use of vivid imagery. And they also, eventually, do more than merely shape attitudes; they can also shape behavior. If you doubt this, simply ask yourself why companies were willing to pay $2.5 million *per minute* to advertise during last year's Academy Awards. The answer is that giant corporations know that what is seen and heard can affect behavior, in this case the buying behavior of millions of people.

The question is: What sorts of messages have been sent in recent years? Put aside advertising, and the fact that an increasing number of television commercials encourage people to "make your own rules" and "peel off inhibitions." Focus instead on programming.

On many daytime talk shows, indecent exposure is celebrated as a virtue, perversions are made to seem commonplace, and modesty and discretion are frowned upon. Jenny Jones once featured a woman who was impregnated while filming a pornographic video. Sally Jessy Raphael had a guest who claimed over two hundred sexual partners. Montel Williams brought on a woman, eight months pregnant, who boasted of eight sexual partners in her first two trimesters. And although his show is less popular of late, Jerry Springer has a legacy of being the worst, as a few of his episode titles alone attest: "Why Have Sex for Free," "My Sister Slept with My Three Husbands," "I'm a Fourteen-Year-Old Prostitute," "Mom Dated My Classmate."

As for prime-time television, it provides us with a steady diet of (among other things) infidelity, promiscuity, and half-naked bodies groping in bed. Program after program, it keeps lowering the threshold of what is acceptable—to the point where soft porn is now being regularly broadcast by America's major networks and often sponsored by America's major corporations.

Item: In a spoof of a DeBeers commercial, a man presents a woman with a diamond; she kisses him and then appears to kneel before him. Cut to a card, reading, "Diamonds. She'll pretty much have to." (*Family Guy*, Fox)

Item: Susan introduces herself to a male colleague, who says, "Oh, yeah, you're the one bangin' the boss."

Susan: "Actually, when I got the job, I wasn't banging the boss."

Vicki, another colleague: "First, she was bangin' the [boss's] brother. . . ." (*Suddenly Susan*, NBC)

Item: Dawson, a teenage boy: "What are you suggesting?"

Eve, a teenage girl: "Only the obvious. A night of scorching-hot, unbridled, mind-altering sex."

"Just like that? No first date, no months of getting to know each other?"

"Those are small town rituals for small town girls. Face it, Dawson, we're hot for each other." (*Dawson's Creek*, Warner)

Item: "So what happened to Gordon?"

"I wanted a threesome and he freaked." (*Love and Money*, CBS)

Item: Drew pulls aside his girlfriend, a handywoman, asking her to explain a matchbook, hotel key, and condom in her possession. She responds, "I am fixing a restaurant which is in a hotel."

"And the condom?"

"I thought you'd want to put it on your penis when you thank me for the big screen TV." (*The Drew Carey Show*, ABC)

Item: "She may be taking my popcorn, but she knows there is more in my lap than that." (*That '70s Show*, Fox)

And so it goes, the wit every bit as dreary as the sex is degraded. Nor have I even begun to catalog the violence, the mayhem and destruction, on offer in prime time, which is a subject unto itself. Whenever protests are raised about any of this, the representatives of television and the movies and their defenders in the press invariably reply: Please don't blame the messenger, all we're doing is giving the public what the public wants. And besides, we don't create reality, we only reflect it. And besides, images and dialogue are only images and dialogue. They are essentially harmless; they do not cause anything to happen.

Well, I would hardly go so far as to draw a direct, monocausal connection between what the mass media put out and the crack-up of any individual marriage or relationship, any more than a violence-filled movie (or television program or video game) by itself causes a viewer to arm himself and go out and kill. But the cumulative effect of these things—in conjunction with others—can and does make a difference. This is surely one of the lessons of the Columbine High School killings, themselves broadcast across the nation for all to see.

In one of the secret videos recorded before that massacre, Dylan Klebold sits in an easy chair. Resting on his lap is a sawed-off shotgun he calls Arlene, after a favorite character in the *Doom* video game. In anticipation of their murderous assault, Eric Harris says on tape: "It's going to be like f—ing *Doom*. Tick, tick, tick, tick . . . Haa! That f—ing shotgun is straight out of *Doom*!"

Life imitating art? People who have no trouble advocating that cigarette commercials be banned from the airwaves on the grounds that they encourage young people to smoke should think again about the degree to which all people, and especially young people, take the media's other well-crafted, market-tested messages to heart. The mass media have power precisely because they tap into real human appetites, passions, temptations. They succeed because we are sentient creatures, and because of the tropism of the human heart toward self-indulgence.

Television, the movies, and the world of advertising are the sites in our culture where the most powerful forces of the imagination are harnessed to produce some of the most effective symbolic devices ever seen or heard. Those who work in these media, however sophomoric their own imaginations, play a Promethean role—they hold the fire that ignites hearts and minds.

I want to underscore one point: My concern is less that the messages being sent are antifamily per se (though, with few exceptions, the traditional family is portrayed on prime-time television in an unfavorable, not to say derisory, light). Rather, what is being promoted is an *ethic* that is inimical to marriage and family life. And that ethic is advanced not simply by the leftist denizens of Beverly Hills but by Madison Avenue corporate executives, many of whom undoubtedly vote Republican and lament the reprehensible state of our culture.

IX

Which takes us to the last items on my list of contributing factors. Living in an extraordinarily affluent society can create its own special set of pressures. The more we attain, the more we want. We become captive to our own expectations, and soon our desires are transmuted into "needs," calling to mind Reinhold Niebuhr's aphorism that human desires increase with the means of their gratification.

This, too, has had a powerful impact on the American family. In order to secure our hold on worldly comforts, we spend more time at work and less time with family. Wealth and luxury, in turn, often make it harder to deny the quest for instant gratification, and therefore harder to live *within* the family.

Am I then against the market economy, or against capitalism? Hardly. Capitalism has created a degree of opportunity unimaginable only a few generations ago. While lifting an unprecedented number of people out of poverty, moreover, the free market and private property have also helped to further political freedom and to secure basic human rights. The market economy rewards human initiative, creativity, and excellence. It is, quite simply, the most efficient and humane economic system the world has ever known.

As usual, our founding fathers got things just about right. Capitalism, they saw, was a crucial component in sustaining a liberal, democratic society. But there were also certain human qualities that needed to be disciplined, tamed, and checked: avarice, excessive individualism, the tendency to reduce everything to the economic bottom line, the danger of being entrapped by the enchantments of this world. "Will you tell me how to prevent riches from producing luxury?" John Adams asked Thomas Jefferson. "Will you tell me how to prevent luxury from producing effeminacy, intoxication, extravagance, vice and folly?"

The *family*, it was believed by our founders, would serve as something of a counterbalance to the free market by anchoring people in a different set of values. Men, in particular, if they were both husbands and fathers, would act more responsibly, with greater discipline. But today, the values of the market have encroached on the separate sphere of family life. As Christopher Lasch pointed out, when money becomes the universal measure of value, then motherhood, which after all is unpaid labor, will come to bear the stigma of social inferiority. More broadly, the values of capitalism, with the premium it places on acquisitiveness, competitiveness, "creative destruction," "rational choice," innovation, and self-interest, are often incompatible with and may even be antithetical to the qualities important to marriage and family life—sympathy and deep devotion, patience and restraint, the deferral of gratification, loyalty, and the willingness to lay aside self-interest.

But I must also immediately qualify these remarks. Even if I am right about the potentially adverse affects of the free market ethic, there are free market economies that do not suffer our own particular woes. Look at Singapore and Japan—two countries that are extremely capitalistic and yet culturally far less individualistic and expressive than ours, far more formal and disciplined. Moreover, countries like Japan and South Korea have among the lowest rates of divorce and out-of-wedlock births in the world.

And, for a counterexample from the opposite direction, look at Scandinavia. There, capitalism has long been tempered by a thoroughgoing commitment to the redistribution of wealth and the provision of government sponsored, "cradle-to-grave" social services. Yet, as a recent report in *The Los Angeles Times* noted, Scandinavians have virtually given up on marriage as a framework for family living, preferring cohabitation even after their children are born. According to the article, "With so many couples breaking up, Scandinavians have fallen into patterns of serial monogamy."

In short, if capitalism is a factor in the breakdown of marriage and the family, it is so only by reason of its complicity with other, primarily cultural, factors. "Our ultimate definition of freedom is to do your own thing, to be independent and not rely on anyone, even on spouses," says Berger J. Hareide, director of the Marriage and Family Research Center near Oslo. Norway's minister for children and family affairs, while proud that the Scandinavian nations have brought women into the workforce and created a strong social safety net, believes that these very achievements have harmed the traditional nuclear family. "We are becoming too selfish. I don't think we work hard enough on the relationships between men and women. It's too easy nowadays to meet and go off with a new partner."

For our anticapitalist critics, these are words to ponder.

X

There is a final argument about capitalism and the family that needs to be disposed of. To some on the American Left, the breakdown of the American family is traceable neither to affluence nor to Scandinavian-style egalitarianism run amok, but to their opposites: economic deprivation and social *in*equality, including a decline in job prospects and real income, wage stagnation, and an unraveling social safety net. The author Stephanie Coontz writes that "the increased visibility of economic and social inequities, and the refusal of politicians to address them," are having an acidic effect on the family.

Unfortunately, anyone who insists that poverty and inequality have been the driving engine of family dissolution has to face some inconvenient facts, the first of which is that the decline of marriage and the American family happened during one of the greatest periods of economic *expansion* ever seen on earth. During that expansion, moreover, total social spending by all levels of government, measured in constant 1990 dollars, rose from $143 billion in 1960 to $787 billion in the mid-1990s, a greater than fivefold increase, while means-tested spending on welfare increased by sevenfold. Today, the poverty rate is far below what it was in 1960. Not only do poor people in America have a higher standard of living than middle-class Americans of previous generations but, per capita, they are far wealthier than many people living in Third World countries—where, as it happens, you find mostly intact families.

Consider, too, that in the early part of this century—long before the great civil rights acts of the 1960s—the vast majority of black children lived in two-parent homes. At that time the black family was relatively stable. Today, by contrast, nearly eighty percent of black women will be heads of family at some point in their childbearing years. Similarly, during the Great Depression, when unemployment rates in general exceeded twenty-five percent, you did not see anything like the rate of family breakup we see now; to the contrary, American families famously pulled together. So the theory that economic hard times are driving the fragmentation of the American family flies in the face of an avalanche of data.

Then there is the notion that the restructuring of our economy that enabled the expansion to occur has itself created new forms of instability and social inequality. For Stephanie Coontz, it is not the sexual revolution or any "willful abandonment of responsibility and commitment" that accounts for the dramatic rise in, for example, illegitimacy, but, rather, the "eclipse of traditional employment centers, destruction of formerly high paid union jobs, expansion of the female and minority workforce, and mounting dilemmas of welfare capitalism."

But as the historian Francis Fukuyama has gently pointed out: "The idea that such large changes in social norms could be brought on by economic deprivation in countries that [are] wealthier than any others in human history" should be enough in itself to "give one pause." Of course economic and material conditions affect family and marriage; this has been true throughout history. But it is a species of economic determinism—and of moral blindness—to regard the crack-up of the American family as the exclusive result of material deprivation, and at this particular moment in history it is wholly irrational.

XI

As I have tried to show, the crisis that has overtaken American family life since 1960 cannot be reduced to any single cause, being the outcome, rather, of a whole congeries of elements that have mutually reinforced and built on each other to bring us to our present calamitous pass. If there is any small comfort to be had from this survey of where we are and how we got here, it is that despite the deniers among us, a number of important scholars and thinkers from different political perspectives, some of whose work I have drawn upon in this chapter, have come to grips with the truth of our situation. This is at least a start on the long path toward restoration.

There are other small comforts. Given the extent of the wreckage, one might expect that people in general would be less likely to regard marriage and family as central life goals. But that is not the case: In the words of the sociologist Norval Glenn: "Marriage remains very important to adult Americans [even as] the proportion of Americans married has declined and the proportion successfully married has declined even more." This is not quite the paradox it may seem. What has changed is not the importance we ascribe to marriage and family; what has changed is our understanding of what they are or have become, and also our estimation of the value of commitment, or how long we figure we will *stay* in a marriage and as part of a family.

Amid all the change and tumult, in other words, some things— some aspirations—remain constant. Nor, I hasten to add, is change itself always and necessarily synonymous with decline: The greater equality between the sexes in marriage is one of the most significant and welcome advances of modern times. But in raising the issue of constancy and change, I am already anticipating the theme of my next chapter, in which I mean to put in much wider perspective the astonishing human achievement represented by the emergence of the modern nuclear family—the very achievement now under mortal threat from within.

The Family in History

I

Maybe, conjectured the highly respected *Economist* magazine not very long ago, the current turmoil in the family is nothing new, and nothing to be alarmed about. "Maybe today's Western family, in all of its many jumbled forms—one-parent-headed, second-time-around-headed, grandparent-headed, peopled with half siblings or stepsiblings, or combinations thereof—is simply returning to the complex, diverse state in which in fact [the family] spent most of the last millennium."

After all, continued *The Economist*, human societies did quite well before the advent of the modern nuclear family. And since, as we have learned from our decades-long experiment with different arrangements, all variations of the family and all "combinations thereof" are essentially equivalent, the "unprecedented burst of agonizing in Western society about the collapse of the family" may be completely uncalled for.

The Economist is usually thought to be conservative in its views;

in economics, it often is. But the radically *un*conservative sentiments I have just quoted reveal just how deeply the "anything goes" attitude has penetrated the mind of a normally stringent publication. When it comes to the family, the new conventional wisdom is that in effect there *is* no such thing, and, except for a brief anomalous moment in our history, there never really was; there have only been "families," and no particular form of them is better than any other. So what are we—what am I—worried about?

As it happens, every single point in *The Economist*'s statement is wrong. Wrong as to the direction of history in the "last millennium," wrong as to what is happening at the moment, and wrong, I trust, as to the future. But to see how and why it is wrong, we need to back up a little, for we cannot understand our present situation without reference to the past. In his 1986 Jefferson Lecture, the philosopher Leszek Kolakowski said we study history "to know who we are," and what we are responsible for. In that sense, the study of history has deep practical importance, allowing us to glean wisdom from those who have gone before, including from their mistakes.

In one limited sense, *The Economist* has a point: The modern nuclear family—what is sometimes mistakenly called the "traditional" family—did not appear spontaneously in the long-ago, but, rather, was built up gradually, shaped and molded by human experience. But if both marriage and family life have undergone change over the ages, as indeed they have, this hardly means that the twentieth-century family is an arbitrary construct. There has been a *tendency* of change, change in a certain direction. More: Just as certain characteristics of the family have been malleable, adjusting to times and trends, other aspects, tethered as they are to deep human realities, have remained largely fixed and timeless. This, too, we learn from history, which in the end yields a picture of the "traditional" family that is much more subtle—and more surprising—than easy stereotypes would suggest.

The historical study of the family is a relatively new discipline in our universities, and it has occasioned spirited debate. The scarcity of sources from earlier periods means that scholars must guard against the temptation to speak with absolute certitude. Regrettably, not all have resisted the temptation. I have their cautionary example in mind as I proceed in the following pages to offer a brief sketch of the family during key periods of Western history.

Notice the word "Western." Although there is much to be learned from non-Western cultures, our own society is a product of Western civilization and our institutions acquired their shape through the course of Western history. During that history, moreover, and especially over the last one thousand years, both the pace and character of change have been much more dramatic in the West than elsewhere. The sheer, stunning success of Western civilization is intimately and reciprocally linked with the development of Western family patterns, so much so that it is not always possible to distinguish changes that have taken place as a result of material progress from those that have occurred as a result of shifts in teachings, ideas, and sentiments. Accordingly, in what follows I will sometimes shift from describing social and cultural conditions to taking up the intellectual and moral implications of doctrines and ideas, and vice versa. Though a social scientist—or a theologian—might frown, this rather eclectic method yields, I hope, benefits in understanding and perspective.

I mean to look at five distinct periods in the history of the West, highlighting attitudes and practices that typify their time—and that also challenge certain of our own prevailing assumptions. Broadly speaking, what we shall see over time is the slow easing or diminishment of the purely functional or economic roles of the family and the replacement of necessity with feeling and sentiment as the basis of family life. That the development of the monogamous nuclear family has engendered new problems and tensions is obvious enough; but it is, in and of itself, an enormous, precious, and extremely hard-won human achievement, and one whose character we need to grasp before we blithely toss it aside.

II

Why are there families among humans but not among apes? There is, after all, monogamy (at least to some degree) among primates. But the *human* family is unique. Why is this so? In part it is obviously because humans are born less developed than other mammals, and require years of care, nurture, and structure. But beyond simple reproduction and nurturance, the human family is also the arena in which moral understanding is shaped. In the interaction among family members, by example and precept and habit, are forged such qualities as trust, sympathy, and conscience.

Without these capacities, which come first and foremost from the home, society itself would be impossible. "The family is the association established by nature for the supply of our everyday wants," wrote Aristotle. Out of it, and in connection with other families, comes first the village, then the larger community, and finally the state, "originating in the bare needs of life but continuing in existence for the sake of a good life." But it all begins with the "union of those who cannot exist without each other, namely, male and female."

We are, in short, a "pair-bonding" species. Biological parents come together in a marriage marked by ritual and ceremony, and play the key roles in raising their children. Those two roles complement one another, arising as they do out of the natural complementarity of the sexes. The family is where "socialization"—the generational transmission of moral and cultural values—takes place. And the family is the child's most important model in terms of how life ought to be lived, the setting where children see vivid demonstrations of love, kindness, compassion, generosity, patience, duty, fidelity.

It is in the Hebrew Bible, or Old Testament, with its unforgettable tales of patriarchs and kings, that we see some of these themes played out in a literary source of great antiquity and unsparing honesty. Although ancient Israel was a tribal society, the stories in the Bible make it clear that in it were incubated many of the ethical qualities associated with the family that are vital to what we in the West have become. Mindful of these qualities, indeed, some of today's strongest advocates of "traditional family values" tend to assume that the nuclear family *derives* from the biblical period. Interestingly enough, their opponents agree with them, although they count it as yet another mark against those benighted folk who (in the words of the columnist Anthony Lewis) "want to substitute their vision of a religious polity for the secular system . . . that has made America strong and free."

But neither party is correct. As the scholar Rodney Clapp has pointed out, though the vast majority of ancient Israelites were monogamous, polygamy,* at least among the wealthier, was a commonly accepted practice. And this was but one of the characteristics of the Hebrew family that in Clapp's words, "radically set it apart from our . . . traditional family."

In ancient Israel, as in most other ancient societies, the family was multigenerational and resembled nothing so much as a small

---

* In ancient times, polygamy was thought to be essential to help families increase in size, maintain their property, and provide manpower for military service. Throughout most of human history, polygamy has been, for some, socially unobjectionable, though in the West, monogamy has been the more frequent practice.

village; the average Hebrew household, for example, numbered somewhere between fifty and one hundred people. The family was also patriarchal: Fathers exercised almost complete control over the lives of their children (though the Bible in its candid and unblinking way has caustic things to say about the fathers' frequent failures in this regard). Marriages were often arranged, and these arrangements were driven by social, economic, or political considerations. It was not uncommon for men of a certain class to keep one or more concubines, particularly if their wives proved unable to conceive. Sarah, for example, who was barren before the birth of Isaac, gave her handmaid Hagar to Abraham; Jacob married two sisters, Rachel and Leah; Esau had three wives.

There was more. A wife's primary duty to her husband was procreation; she had few legal rights, could not inherit property upon the death of her husband (it went to his sons), and, though she might take a strong position as an adviser on family matters, addressed him as a servant would address a master. Some women in the Bible did play prominent *public* roles—Deborah, Esther, Jael, and even the wicked Athaliah come to mind—but these were clearly the exceptions.

Children were considered a great blessing and were generally well loved. Still, a father held the power of life and death over his children (though later Mosaic law would restrict that power). And the position of a daughter was clearly inferior to that of a son, particularly a firstborn son who, according to the law of primogeniture, received a double portion of the estate as his birthright.

These are arrangements that, needless to say, modern Americans find unacceptable, violating as they do our understandings of equality, justice, and the role of consent in marriage. But one must be careful in assessing a society that existed three thousand or more years ago. A culture that looks reactionary to modern eyes may turn out to have been enlightened and advanced compared to other civilizations of the same period.

For example, the ancient Hebrews made an enormous contribution to the ancient world's understanding of human sexuality—and, more specifically, to the channeling of sexual activity into marriage. The social critic Dennis Prager reminds us how thoroughly sexuality infused virtually every society of the ancient world. In Greek culture, boys could have intercourse with slaves, prostitutes, or one another. The Jewish people made marriage the sexual ideal—even if, as the Bible frankly informs us, they did not always live up to that ideal. They also elevated the status of women by standing firmly for marriage and the family and firmly against infidelity and homosexuality. Indeed, "throughout their history," writes Prager, echoing many observers over the centuries, "one of the Jews' most distinguishing characteristics has been their commitment to family life."

In addition, the Hebrew Bible desexualized God and religion. In most ancient civilizations—including Babylon, Canaan, Egypt, Greece, and Rome—the gods were "extremely promiscuous, both with other gods and with mortals." As a result, religions themselves were thoroughly sexualized. Judaism changed all that.

What about love? While many biblical marriages were arranged, it was believed that love would develop between husband and wife. Ecclesiastes instructs us to "enjoy life with the wife whom you love, all the days of your fleeting life which He has given you under the sun," and elsewhere we are told: "Let your fountain be blessed, and rejoice in the wife of your youth." The Bible includes (in the book of Proverbs) a beautiful, stirring tribute to the good wife, the "woman of valor," and Genesis teaches that a man is made whole when he becomes "one flesh" with his wife.

From the time of the Bible on, the Jewish tradition also placed great emphasis on honoring one's parents; many ancient rabbis considered the commandment to honor parents the greatest in the law—similar to honoring God. And this is a God, remember, who, in contrast to the pagan gods, exemplified in His own actions the domestic ideal. In the pithy words of Huston Smith, a leading authority on the history of religion, "Whereas the gods of Olympus tirelessly pursued beautiful women, the God of Sinai watched over widows and orphans. . . . God is a God of righteousness, whose loving kindness is from everlasting to everlasting and whose tender mercies are in all His works."

It bears saying once again: Much that was taken for granted about family life in ancient Israel is contrary to present-day belief and, for good reasons, unacceptable to us. But much—especially the very conception of the family as the seedbed of moral refinement and individual growth—is already there, not hidden away but right out in the open, waiting to be further developed.

III

Western civilization has been influenced beyond measure by Christianity, from the ethical teachings of Jesus to the doctrines of patristic and later authorities to the evolving institutional practices of the Church and the community of the faithful. Christianity's impact on the family, and on our ideas about the family, has been incalculable.

When the teachings of Jesus and the New Testament were written down, the Romans had already inaugurated new understandings of life in society. In pagan Rome, systems of religious belief other than the official one were under a grant of (limited) tolerance, at least so long as they did not present a direct challenge to prevailing authority. At the same time, Roman law had codified the obligations of family members to one another, and monogamy was the norm.

But whatever the law might proclaim, Imperial Rome was also

entering into a state of dissolution that would last for several centuries, while in other societies around the Mediterranean, the Roman ethos had not made significant inroads into older customs and attitudes. The status of women is a good example. In most cultures, it had slowly improved since more primitive days, but selectively and often superficially. Roman matrons of the higher classes (but only of the higher classes) were well respected, might assist their husbands in business, and sometimes managed their own property. Among Jewish women, some were active and engaged in society—including in religious leadership. Still, these tended to be the exceptions: In virtually every culture in the first century, women's social standing in general was low, and opportunities to advance almost nonexistent; worse, women were held to be inferior to men and thought to be responsible for sexual sin.

It was in this context that Jesus lived, thought, and exercised his profound effect on all of later history. His attitude toward women, a measure of much else about him and the faith he preached, incidentally gives the lie to those who stubbornly continue to believe that Christianity is "about" the subjugation and suppression of women. Jesus treated women with a much higher regard than was common at the time, and his example eventually helped to shape the Christian understanding of male-female relationships, marriage, and family life. (Which is not to say that the Christian Church has always lived up to the example of its founder.) Women were among Jesus' close followers, playing a major role in his ministry and in the spreading of his gospel, and serving as positive models in his teachings. Jesus praised their faith, and graciously accepted their acts of love and hospitality. It was women who were the first eyewitnesses of his resurrection and who were then told to go and relate the news to the male disciples. Mary, the mother of Jesus, was specially favored by God.

Jesus held men and women alike to the same moral standards—

in his Sermon on the Mount, he accounted *men*, not women, responsible for lust, something very unusual in ancient Mediterranean cultures—and taught that all must follow the same path to salvation. This precept clearly influenced his followers. St. Paul, for example, penned what in first-century Palestine must have been a stunningly egalitarian sentiment: "There is neither Jew nor Greek, slave nor free, *male nor female,* for you are all one in Christ Jesus" (emphasis added). Paul was not implying here that men and women were the same in every regard, nor was he denying that men and women had unique and complementary roles to play within marriage; his own writings make that clear enough. Rather, he was making the point that unity in Christ transcends ethnic, social, and sexual distinctions—a point that in itself accorded a higher status to women than heretofore.

What of the New Testament's attitude toward the family? It turns out to be more complicated than many people imagine. On the one hand, the family is spoken of in exceedingly high, even holy, terms. The husband-wife relationship is invoked by Paul to describe the relationship between Christ and the Church, his "bride." Husbands are told to love their wives just as Christ loved the Church, and husbands and wives are urged to submit to one another out of reverence for Christ. The vow of marriage is meant to be permanent, enduring, indissoluble; divorce was to be exceedingly rare, permissible only on grounds of adultery and desertion. In the New Testament Church, one of the prerequisites for leadership was a man's wise stewardship of his own family.

In a usage borrowed from the Hebrew Bible, Jesus and Paul refer to God as *abba,* "father." The proof of God's love for us, we learn, is that all of us have been given the right to be called "children of God." Earthly children are especially blessed; they have a share in the kingdom of God, and are often held up as examples for those who would enter that kingdom. And just as all humans are bound to honor and obey God, so children are instructed to honor and obey their parents, while fathers are expected to raise their children with wisdom and care, "in the training and instruction of the Lord."

But an honest assessment of the New Testament also finds curious contradictions and tensions. Jesus repeatedly warned that he would be the cause of enmity and division between parents and children, as well as among siblings and in-laws. Family ties are often portrayed in New Testament teachings as less important, and less enduring, than ties to the community of fellow believers. Indeed, the family is itself sometimes viewed with suspicion, for the radical missionary summons of Jesus requires individuals to leave everything, including their loved ones and occupations, to follow the Lord. In Corinthians, Paul appears to endorse a single life over marriage—albeit a life in the community of the faithful.

Where to strike the balance? The New Testament is hardly antifamily, nor does the Christian faith ask us to devalue family loyalty. Rather, it insists that there is something that transcends *even* family relationships. Family life, while vitally important, ought not be idolized; everything must finally be placed in its right order.

But that is not the whole story, either. The same Paul who in Corinthians endorses the single life also authored the tribute to marriage we find in Ephesians. What Jesus plainly believed is that it is right for some, if not most, people to devote themselves to family life, even as some are urged to leave everything behind and follow him. Individual talents, needs, and circumstances play a part in how people of faith live out their lives, and although loyalty to God must take preference over loyalty to family, it is (in the words of one commentator) "virtually the *only* justification for family disloyalty."

Honest appraisal of the New Testament may well tell us something hard to accept in our gilded age, namely, that there is, for serious Christians, a real cost to discipleship—a "radical detachment . . . from possessions, from family ties, and even from one's own spouse." The demands of Christian faith can reach farther than many of us sometimes want to admit. At the same time, the *ideal* of sacrificial love is a deeply inspiring one, and it does, after all, constitute perhaps the most solid foundation for family life.

In sum, the relationship of religious faith to marriage and family life is complex and at times paradoxical. If that reminds us, as it should, of the difficulties in any effort to turn either the Hebrew Bible or the New Testament into a straightforward brief for traditional "family values," it should also remind us of how rich, how demanding, and how endlessly instructive is the moral and spiritual legacy we are heirs to.

IV

The Middle Ages, the transition period from antiquity to the modern world, is a huge historical terrain marked by the fragmentation of the Roman Empire, the growth and influence of the Roman Catholic Church, the spread and then the collapse of feudalism, and the rise of nationalism and the European states. Reconstructing family life during the millennium from A.D. 500 to 1500 is therefore a treacherous undertaking. To make matters still harder, the documentary evidence is often fragmentary and incomplete—"far less diverse and less abundant," as one historian has put it, "than that for Roman antiquity."

At the dawn of the European Middle Ages, a key role was played by extended family and kin relatives: brothers, sisters, grandparents, uncles, aunts, nieces, nephews, distant cousins. The nuclear family—father, mother, children—was "no more than a loose core at the center of a dense network of lineage and kin relationships," and family life was, therefore, far from a private affair. Nor was the family much of a haven, a place in which to seek solace from the world outside. Indeed, marriage itself was at least as much about a pathway to a new and larger kinship community as it was about a deep, intimate relationship with one's spouse.

This dynamic would change over the thousand-year span of the Middle Ages. By the end of the period, permanent, monogamous marriage had triumphed, and home was more comforting and more private. While the family remained, in the words of the scholars Frances and Joseph Gies, "society's fundamental building block," both Romans and barbarians "would have found marriage and the family in 1500 radically different from what they had known."

What accounted for the change was in large measure the formative, and formidable, influence of Church law and teachings. Never before the Middle Ages, and never since, has a religious institution played so prominent a role in Western society. The Church affected virtually every corner of medieval life—including, mightily, attitudes toward marriage and sex. As the Gieses put it, "In the year 500 the Church could only protest and admonish; in the year 1000 it could threaten and command." By the twelfth century, canon law had "eclipsed secular jurisprudence on all matters relating to marriage."

In the first few centuries of Christianity, marital sex had been accepted by Church authorities as both "the most exquisite of physical pleasures and a civic duty in order to reproduce the species." But by the fourth century, official views began to change, and celibacy came to be viewed as a superior state to marriage—a doctrine resting, as we have seen, on Paul's teaching in Corinthians. ("Now to the unmarried and the widows I say: It is good for them to stay unmarried, as I am. But if they cannot control themselves, they should marry, for it is better to marry than to burn with passion.") This doctrine was institutionalized in the celibate priesthood, and there was thus initiated a bias toward celibacy in canon law. In the fullness of time, this notion of marriage as a second-best option would form one of the reasons that Protestant reformers rebelled against the Catholic Church.

The Church's views on sex had been shaped largely by the thinking of the early church fathers, many of whom were deeply mistrustful of the pleasure that accompanied sexual intercourse, believing that it turned people away from spiritual contemplation, self-control, and obedience, and toward idolatry, worldliness, and the dark side of human nature.* St. Ambrose, one of the most illustrious figures of the early church, wrote that "married people ought to blush at the state in which they are living." To St. Augustine the passion accompanying marital sex was sinful even if the sexual act itself was not. As the historian Lawrence Stone has dramatically summed up:

> From the third to the tenth century, the Church authorities issued edicts forbidding sex for religious reasons on Saturdays, Sundays, Wednesdays, and Fridays—and for the 40-day fast periods before Easter, Christmas, and Witsuntide. Some writers added major feast days of the Church and the days of the Apostles to the proscription. To these were added

---

* It is important to note that the attitudes of the Catholic Church toward human sexuality have shifted dramatically since the Middle Ages. Pope John Paul II, for instance, has written about the beauty and power of conjugal love. And while the Catholic Church still adheres to the elevation of virginity above marriage, it certainly views marriage as a positive good. Indeed, John Paul II has made it clear that virginity's value does not flow from its rejection of pleasure of the flesh but, rather, resides in its dedication to the spiritual life. "The 'superiority' of continence to marriage," he has written, "never means disparagement of matrimony or belittlement of its essential value.... We do not find any basis whatever for any disparagement of matrimony."

the days of female impurity (menstruation, pregnancy, a month after delivery, even while breast-feeding). If all these injunctions had been obeyed, the number of days a year on which marital sex was permitted would have been reduced to between 21 and 44.

If marriage was considered an inferior state to celibacy, the Church also strongly held to the view that as an institution ordained by God, the married state offered the *only* framework under which children ought to be conceived and born. The primary purpose of sex was procreation, while masturbation and homosexuality were to be severely penalized. Over the course of the medieval period, the Roman Catholic Church was influential in prohibiting incest and the marrying of close relatives, in punishing fornication and adultery, and in rendering polygamy and concubinage unacceptable (though the wealthy and powerful sometimes took more than one wife and kept mistresses).

Finally, the Church held that marriage, once contracted, was an indissoluble union. True, Church councils in the latter half of the eighth century had acknowledged some valid grounds for dissolving marriages: "adultery, servile status, leprosy, lack of consent, impotence, one partner's becoming a monk or nun." But divorce by mutual consent was not allowed, and this view dominated throughout the medieval age.

Nevertheless, the Church did champion the role of consent in marriage, marking a historic change from the earlier periods we have examined. While parents and relatives retained final say over the choice of partners, Catholic teaching backed the right of the bride and groom to express their feelings as well. (But of course it would be a long time before compatibility and consent would overtake land or money as the decisive factors in choosing marriage partners.)

As for the attitude toward children, Lawrence Stone reminds us that during the Middle Ages, two or more living children were often given the same name because it was so common that at least one of them would die. If, for almost any parent today, the thought of losing a child is unbearable, that was surely the case for most parents in the Middle Ages too. And yet it was also a reality that many could not escape. This was particularly true during the Black Death, the epidemic that ravaged Europe and Asia in the fourteenth century, and that is estimated to have killed one-quarter or more of the populations of Europe, including, no doubt, a disproportionate number of children. One can only imagine the repercussions on family life—including on the emotional investment parents could allow themselves to make in children who might be cruelly taken from their midst.

These last considerations form a necessary background to understanding one salient characteristic of the era: the rather common and, to us, stunning practice of child abandonment. In the Middle Ages, parents suffered no serious sanctions for deserting their children; indeed, the practice was permitted by civil and Church authorities alike. According to the late John Boswell, "Children were abandoned throughout Europe from Hellenistic antiquity to the end of the Middle Ages in great numbers, by parents of every social standing, in a great variety of circumstances."

Large-scale abandonment has, to be sure, a rather long history in the West. It was often seen as a matter of simple economic necessity, and as such did not appear to raise many moral objections. Indeed, by the time of the Middle Ages, things may actually have improved somewhat, in the sense that the *child's* welfare seems to have become a chief concern, especially for families in the lower classes who now had reason to hope that in other hands their children might lead better lives. To this end, a relatively humane method was put into place.

During the High Middle Ages, churches increasingly served as depositories for abandoned children, and the concept eventually arose of an oblation, or offering, in which a child would be donated as a permanent gift to a monastery. (St. Thomas Aquinas, among the greatest theologians in history, was an oblate at age six.) In other instances, abandoned children were taken in by barren couples. Thanks to the "kindness of strangers," it is estimated that abandoned infants died at only a slightly higher rate than was normal for all infants during the period.

But tender mercies did not always prevail. Horrifying is not too strong a word for the fate that befell many children, especially in earlier periods, a fate that could include being sold into slavery, prostitution, castration, and mutilation. In ancient Rome, whose literature is filled with expressions of parental affection toward children, infanticide was a widespread and accepted practice among the poor. And even later, whether out of economic need or for other reasons, many adults considered children surplus, unwanted burdens. Nor did matters necessarily improve with the rise in the fourteenth century and later of foundling hospitals. In such institutions, overcrowding, disease, poor hygiene, and general neglect led to a mortality rate as high as ninety percent.

Today we react with horror when we read about young couples abandoning infants in garbage bins; we deem it a barbaric, almost an unthinkable, act. We are right to do so. But we should bear in mind that unwanted children have always been with us; and so, too, have such barbaric acts. It turns out—history teaches us—that a civilization placing a premium on natality, welcoming all children into life, is not as common an achievement as we might think.

V

The period from roughly 1500 through the mid-1700s serves as a watershed. During this tumultuous era—sometimes referred to as the "early modern" age—one can see both the lingering influence of the Middle Ages and portents of things to come. Among those portents were, in shorthand, the Protestant Reformation, a growing dissatisfaction with monarchy and religious orthodoxy that would lead eventually to the separation of spiritual from temporal power, demands for more representative government, the advent of modern capitalism, and other manifestations of the individualism that has given its stamp to the modern West. This was also the period that saw the rise of the first American families, which, with their roots in English Puritanism, soon came to be considered an American ideal.

The Puritan family was usually quite large, with eight to ten children per married couple. It was nuclear in its structure, patriarchal, and intimately connected to the surrounding community. Because it was self-sufficient and took upon itself so many different tasks, it was also often referred to as a "little commonwealth." One can see why: The Puritan household was the place where parents taught children to read, the workshop where most furniture was built and most clothing was made, a place of worship, a hospice for the sick and aged, and a vocational center and "house of correction."

In all these senses, the family was, still, vastly different from the institution to which we are now accustomed, with its focus on the themes of personal relations and emotional intimacy. Indeed, it has been argued by some scholars that in the early colonies, marital relations themselves tended to be functional, cool, emotionally distant, and relatively unromantic. But others disagree, pointing to the emphasis placed by the Puritans on married affection, companionship, and fidelity.

Unlike the position of the Church in the Middle Ages, the Puritans did not believe that "celibacy was a condition morally superior to marriage." Rather, marriage was seen as a holy union, and the purpose of marital sex included mutual comfort and tenderness as well as procreation. In short, within the Puritan marriage relationship itself, one can observe the seeds of the "romantic ideal" that would characterize nineteenth-century marriage in America.

Consider the relationship between John Winthrop, the seventeenth-century governor of the Massachusetts Bay Colony, and his wife, Margaret. In his book *At Odds,* the historian Carl N. Degler cites the words of Mrs. Winthrop to her husband on the two chief reasons she loves him: "first because thou lovest God; and, secondly, because that thou lovest me. If these two were wanting, all the rest would be eclipsed." Governor Winthrop held his wife in similar esteem, writing to her: "The largeness and truth of my love to thee makes me always mindful of thy welfare and sets me on work to begin to write before I hear from thee. The very thought of thee affords me many a kind refreshment: What will then be the enjoying of thy sweet society, which I prize above all worldly comforts?" One might also quote from the poems of Anne Bradstreet, considered by many to be the first important woman writer in America: "To my Dear and loving Husband/I prise thy love more than whole Mines of gold."

During the seventeenth century, the position of women in marriage seems to have improved—if only to a point. A wife was still expected to be submissive and compliant, a helpmate and not an equal. An essential but secondary part of the family, she was responsible for domestic duties and care of the home, supervising servants and apprentices, keeping financial records, providing nurture to infants and young children. She had few legal rights apart from her husband, and, upon marriage, all property she owned was turned over to him.

The Puritan father, on the other hand, believed that his near-absolute authority had been delegated by God. The unquestioned ruler of the family, he was often authoritarian, stern, strict, quick to intervene in the lives of his children, a disciplinarian who would dispense sometimes harsh physical punishment. Yet it would be a mistake to conclude from this—as some do—that Puritan fathers did not enjoy a deep emotional bond with their children. In fact, seventeenth-century Puritans, fathers and mothers alike, "cared deeply for their children and invested an enormous amount of time and energy in them." In the view of the scholar John Demos, the devotion of Puritan fathers to their children has not since been equaled.

Take the attitude toward newborn children in seventeenth-century New England. Many Puritans, adopting the strict Calvinist perspective, considered them products of original sin: inherently corrupt, naturally depraved. The role of a responsible parent, therefore, was to reshape the child's will through discipline, instruction, admonition, and moral education. "Surely there is in all children (though not alike) a stubbernes and stoutnes of minde arrising from naturall pride," said one Puritan pastor, "which must in the first place be broken and beaten down."

But if parents sometimes went to excess—as they surely did—it was not primarily out of callousness or capriciousness; rather, for many Puritans these acts were carried out in a spirit of duty and responsibility, "so the foundation of their education being layd in humilitie and tractablenes" (as our pastor went on), "other virtues may in turn be built thereon." And let us not forget that Puritan adults held themselves, too, to be corrupted by the Fall—that, in the words of Paul, "all have sinned and fallen short of the glory of God."

By the late seventeenth century, Puritanism was beginning to decline in England. The English philosopher John Locke—whose ideas did so much to influence the American founding—played a crucial role in altering public attitudes toward children as well. To Locke (who was not alone in this belief), an infant was less a product of the Fall than a blank slate, a *tabula rasa*. This conception, Lawrence Stone argues, stimulated the display of parental love and affection even if mothers and fathers were still far from viewing childhood as a distinct phase of life with its own special needs and interests.

The historical evidence suggests that over the course of a century and a half—from the early 1600s through the mid-1700s—the Puritan family changed, adapted, and reshaped itself. Steven Mintz and Susan Kellogg write that, during this period, parental authority weakened, fathers and mothers began to indulge children more, household rules were relaxed (for example, children no longer had to stand while their parents ate), children were "fostered out" less frequently, privacy became more important, and real property played a diminished role in deciding who wed whom. In their words:

> A "silent revolution" had taken place, one that diminished parental control over children's marriages, differentiated family patterns across social classes, and produced a new conception of childhood in which children were viewed not as embodiments of sin but as innocent and malleable creatures whose characters could be molded into any shape.

By the end of the colonial period, then, currents were astir that would find their full realization by the early part of the next century.

VI

In the seventeenth century, it was parents who were responsible for arranging marriages while their children were able, in some instances, to exercise a veto. From the late eighteenth century forward, in both the United States and Britain, children of adult age were often allowed to choose their marriage partners, while parents were the ones with the veto power. By the 1830s, the free choice of spouse was seen as "a distinctive feature of American family life."

The basis for marriage changed as well. In previous centuries, property and economic considerations were determinative. By the late eighteenth century, for the first time in history, marriage was seen to rest on voluntary affection and personal happiness, friendship and companionship, love and romance, sexual attraction and personal intimacy.

"For the first time in history": This requires a pause. From everything we have seen until now, it should be clear why I do not accept the proposition, advanced by some historians, that pre-modern marriages, because they were arranged, were loveless affairs. First of all, to those quick to condemn the central role once played by economic considerations, I would urge attention to context. "Though to modern perceptions the economic concerns that preoccupied parties to a marriage in former times seem discordantly mercenary," Frances and Joseph Gies have wisely written, "to families entirely dependent on land for their livelihood such concerns were inevitable and primary." Second of all, people often *learned* to love one another over the life of a marriage.

In that sense, we contemporaries can also learn something useful from our ancestors. Too many people today believe that once a marriage goes flat—once the early love, affection, and intense attraction are gone—a marriage itself is irretrievably broken. In fact, there is plenty of evidence, from the past and from today, that people can fall in love again with their spouses. It may require time, effort, a conscious commitment of purpose, perhaps even outside counsel; but it can be done, and it is almost always worth the effort.

But let us return to the changes afoot in the eighteenth century, one of which was a significant enhancement of the status of women. Though still legally and socially inferior to their husbands, wives were now often perceived as *moral* superiors, purer, less corrupted, and less susceptible to the dangerous allure of wealth, power, and ambition. In the words of Carl Degler, "it was not unusual to refer to women as the 'angels of the house,' for they were said to be the moral guardians of the family." Sarah Josepha Hale, a leading journalist of the time, declared that a woman was "God's appointed agent of MORALITY," responsible for refining a man's "human affections and elevat[ing] his moral feelings."

The emergent nuclear family was also coming to be characterized by the "doctrine of the two spheres," referring to the sharp division of labor between husband and wife. Although single women usually participated in the workforce, upon marriage—and even before motherhood—they were expected to leave that sphere to their husbands and become full-time housewives, directing their energies to taking care of the home and raising children.

Some feminists today have come to view this "domestic tyranny" with utter contempt. But women at the time thought otherwise, taking pride and satisfaction in their domestic role. And in fact the arrangement did benefit women, offering them, in the words of one writer, the "opportunity to wield incomparable power" and "asserting a companionate role" that "implicitly denied patriarchy." The keenest of all observers of American life, Alexis de Tocqueville, noted that while Americans did not believe that "man and woman have either the duty or the right to perform the same offices," they did show "an equal regard for both their respective parts;

and though their lot is different, they consider both of them as beings of equal value." "As for myself," Tocqueville concluded:

> I do not hesitate to avow that although the women of the
> United States are confined within the narrow circle of do-
> mestic life, and their situation is in some respects one of ex-
> treme dependence, I have nowhere seen woman occupying a
> loftier position; and if I were asked . . . to what the singular
> prosperity and growing strength of that people ought
> mainly to be attributed, I should reply: To the superiority of
> their women.

During the nineteenth century, relations between husbands and
wives would appear to have grown progressively less formal and
more expressive, intimate, and warm. In their correspondence, it
was not uncommon for couples to use endearing language and express deep mutual yearnings. ("Sometimes such a feeling of longing
for you, dearest, comes over me that I feel as if I *must* fly to you,"
wrote an absent Mary Poor to her husband in 1846.) It would also
appear that spouses were quite faithful: For American men, there
was no gallantry to be found in a love affair, and women were expected to be chaste. One English visitor, remarking upon the "great
charm which surrounds all family relations in the North," made a
point of recording that "compared with Europe, domestic scandals
are unknown."

During the late eighteenth and nineteenth centuries, too, the
home came to be viewed as a special, almost sanctified place, truly a
"haven in a heartless world." Keep in mind that men were being
drawn away from home and into the marketplace on a mass scale.
The Industrial Revolution forced sweeping changes in every sphere,
shifting people from agrarian to urban settings, creating smaller and
more self-contained family units, and encouraging an unprece-

dented mobility. It took time, and a fair amount of disruptive agony, to adjust to these changes, and in doing so, people tended to draw closer within their families. Men in particular looked more and more to their wives and their homes for emotional support, nurturance, and affirmation.

One late-nineteenth-century female author, E. B. Duffey, captured the spirit of the times in her book, *What Women Should Know*:

> The true home is a world within a world. It is the central point of the universe around which all things revolve. It is the treasure-house of the affections, the one serenely bright spot in all the world, toward which its absent members always look with hope and anticipation.

Concomitantly, an important shift occurred in attitudes toward children and child-rearing. Having by now ceded many of its traditional functions (economic, educational, etc.) to other institutions, the family came to focus more on "the socialization of children and the provision of emotional support and affection." In the words of Christopher Lasch: "Child-rearing ceased to be simply one of many activities and became the central concern—one is tempted to say the central obsession—of family life."

The means by which Americans sought to educate their young morally also changed rather dramatically. According to Mintz and Kellogg:

> There was a growing consensus that the object of child rearing was not to break a child's will through intense moral or physical pressure but to shape his or her character in preparation for the temptations of life.... According to innumerable guidebooks, tracts, and domestic novels dealing with the "art and responsibility of family government," the

formation of character was best achieved . . . by emotional nurture, parental love, and the force of parental example.

Since it was assumed, reasonably enough, that women were better suited to provide the necessary patient love, affection, and affirmation, the result was that in child-rearing the mother became the "primary parent." (It is true, though, that greater attention to children might also increase the likelihood of a mother's loyalty being split, putting strain on her relationship with her husband.) As for fathers, their role evolved as well, with less emphasis on strict discipline and more on tenderness and (particularly in the case of older children) friendship. All this was facilitated by a huge demographic shift, as fertility rates fell by fifty percent.

This entire era—the Victorian era—has often been caricatured as sexually and emotionally repressed, patriarchal, tyrannical, and abusive. In fact, the hallmarks of family life included stability and faithfulness, emotional intimacy, and endurance. Things were not perfect by any means, and there were surely elements that from our vantage point we would want to change. But given the problems that plague *contemporary* family life—out-of-wedlock births and single-parent families, divorce and cohabitation, abortion on demand and the growing embrace of homosexual unions, to name just a few—a bit of humility, not to say appreciativeness, is surely called for.

A final point: The emerging attitudes I have been describing were not rooted in unenlightened, authoritarian, or misogynistic ideals. Rather, they were firmly anchored in the liberal political tradition. This was, after all, an America chiseled and shaped by the ideas of the Enlightenment, in particular by the writings of John Locke and Thomas Jefferson. These ideas, including the notion of "affective individualism," contributed, in the words of family historian Barbara Dafoe Whitehead, "to more egalitarianism in family relationships, a higher level of parental nurture and investment in children, a more affectionate climate in family life . . . [and] a cultural ideal of child-centeredness."

Would that we could say the same of our own age.

VII

Such, then, are a few snapshots of key moments in the history of the family in the West. I believe they are deeply revealing. As we return full circle, one thing impresses me above all: The most important and precious achievements in the realm of marriage and family life have not been the result of mere happenstance. Spurred (or detained) by economic circumstances, they have been primarily the result of trial and error, of accumulated wisdom, and of moral enlightenment—sometimes one, sometimes another, sometimes a combination. Shaped as we are by long human experience, we must be all the more careful not to lose what has required so much time and so much effort to accomplish. The modern nuclear family is a rare construct; we tamper with its essentials at our peril.

With a view toward the lessons of history, then, what changes *ought* we now accommodate—and what changes ought we resist? Put another way: What are the essentials we should fight to preserve?

It might be best to start by acknowledging that certain trends are irreversible. We are not going back—nor should we—to a time when marriages were arranged, marital sex was frowned upon, polygamy was acceptable, children were abandoned on a wide scale, boys were favored in every important way over girls, and women were subjugated and demeaned, or denied participation in the labor force. It is unlikely, too, that we will return to a time when contraception was denied, or people lived within an elaborate kinship network, or the home was the center of economic activity (though today's technology is, in fact, allowing more and more people to work from home and to educate their children at home).

At the same time, we desperately need to reestablish marriage as an exclusive arrangement between a man and a woman that is a place of sexual and emotional intimacy, affection, and friendship. Marriage, monogamous and freely chosen, must be the institution through which children are conceived and born, loved and disciplined, nurtured and raised. And marital *permanence* must once again become the ideal to which individuals commit themselves and which they strive to maintain.

We need to protect the concept of childhood as a distinct and cherished period of life, and of children as deserving the attention and devotion of their parents. And we need to accept the fact that children thrive best when they are cared for by a mother and a father who are committed to each other in a stable and enduring marital relationship. When we as a society move away from the two-parent family and replace it with alternative arrangements, children tend to suffer, often grievously.

We should recognize, too, that while many things about marriage and family life have changed, certain things have remained near-constants, and not just in the West but in almost every culture throughout most of human history. Incest is taboo. Homosexual marriages are not countenanced. Marriage serves as the optimal way to satisfy the sexual needs of men and women. Births out of wedlock are not a cultural norm, and neither are single parents.

Yes, marriage and family arrangements have assumed different forms throughout history. But does that mean we can invent virtually any new arrangement we like and preserve what we have gained, as that quotation from *The Economist* I began with blandly assumes?

Hardly. The *structures* of marriage and family may have been many; the *purposes* are very few. The fundamental task human be-ings face is the preservation and continuity of the human order. This means that we must not only reproduce our species but social-ize our young. For adult humans—unlike, say, for adult lizards—the having of children is but the beginning of the task. For their first few years, children are utterly helpless and wholly dependent on others, and even after that their character, sentiments, and values re-main to be shaped. The moral education of the young has almost al-ways been among the primary duties of parents.

A family structure consisting of a mother, father, and child em-bedded in other, larger and complementary structures is not uncom-mon and may well serve the purpose of assisting and protecting a mother and her offspring in the first few years of life. But what no previous society has ever successfully done, to my knowledge, is to set up a family arrangement that consciously tries, as David Blanken-horn puts it, to break up the *nucleus* of the nuclear family. Some, it is true—as in the early kibbutz and other such communal arrange-ments—have tried to peel away the significance of the family unit, but virtually everywhere this has been tried it has turned out to be harmful to the children involved, or we have seen human nature re-assert itself with mothers and fathers reclaiming their children. The bottom line is that not all family structures are equal, and not all variations are compatible with basic social and human needs. Per-haps without fully grasping it, we are challenging some of the cen-tral and accepted truths of human history. The forms this challenge takes are discrete; they include, among other things, illegitimacy, co-habitation, and fatherlessness; homosexual marriage; and divorce. Each is a very controversial topic, and we shall take each up in turn. But separately and together, they pose a mortal threat.

My concern is that we are now embarked upon an experiment that violates a universal social law: In attempting to raise children without two parents, we are seeing, on a massive scale, the voluntary breakup of the minimal family unit. This is historically unprecedented, an authentic cultural revolution—and, I believe, socially calamitous. We may be under the illusion that we can cheerfully deconstruct marriage and then one day decide to pull back from the brink. But as a friend of mine puts it, once you shoot out the lights, can you shoot them back on again? As the long record of human experimentation attests, civilizations, even great civilizations, are more fragile and perishable than we think.

Cohabitation,
Illegitimacy,
Fatherlessness

I

On October 14, 1996, Madonna Ciccone—the then thirty-eight-year-old pop culture icon—gave birth to a daughter, Lourdes. "This is," she said, "the greatest miracle of my life." Madonna was also a single mother. Fifty years ago, this fact alone would have damaged her career, perhaps irreparably. In the late 1940s, when Ingrid Bergman left her husband and daughter for the director Roberto Rossellini, and bore Rossellini's child before they married, the reaction was swift and fierce: Bergman's films were boycotted, she was essentially banned from Hollywood for years, criticized by women's groups as a bad example, and denounced on the Senate floor as a "powerful influence for evil."

But Madonna was not just forgiven (no question of *that*); she was lionized. "I've never seen her happier," applauded Rosie O'Donnell, while *People* chimed in that Lourdes had "transformed Madonna into her most fulfilling role yet—adoring single mother."

Becoming a single mother had, indeed, solidified her "mystique" as a thoroughly modern, fully independent woman.

A few months after the birth, Madonna was asked about motherhood without marriage. "The most important thing is to have love," she said. "That happens with a marriage, without a marriage, with a single parent, whatever." As for the father of Lourdes, Carlos Leon, who had been the singer's personal trainer in New York, he was reportedly ecstatic at the birth of his child, whom he occasionally traveled to visit in London, where Madonna now makes her home.

In the summer of 2000, Madonna, still unmarried, gave birth to her second child, Rocco, the son of the thirty-one-year-old British director Guy Ritchie. Like Leon, Ritchie, too, was reportedly ecstatic at the birth of his child. "Fatherhood is unbelievable," he said. But Guy Ritchie's father stressed that his son wouldn't "rush into marriage" with Madonna. Finally, in December 2000, Ritchie and Madonna were married.

"Where's Daddy?" was the cover line on the May 4, 1998, special issue of *Sports Illustrated,* focusing on athletes who father children out of wedlock. The story opened with an account of Larry Johnson, star forward of the New York Knicks, arriving at a Long Beach (California) clinic on November 7, 1997, just hours before a game against the Los Angeles Lakers. Johnson was met at the clinic by six people, including Laura Tate, an aspiring model with whom he had conducted a fifteen-month affair, and Tate's three-month-old daughter, Taylor Tate Johnson.

Johnson would rather have been anywhere else that day. According to Ms. Tate, after first learning of her pregnancy, Johnson had called her as often as four times a day urging her to have an abortion. In the clinic's examining room Johnson's blood was drawn; the test showed that he was indeed the father of Taylor. On November 17, a Los Angeles judge ordered Johnson to pay almost $9,000 per month in child support, and $30,000 a year for a nanny.

Nor was this Johnson's first paternity suit. In October 1993, former flight attendant Angela Jeffress gave birth to a child whom DNA tests subsequently determined to be Johnson's as well. Documents indicate that Johnson, in addition to two children he has with his wife Celeste, is now supporting three other children by three other women.

And Johnson is hardly unique; at the time of the *Sports Illustrated* article, a list of NBA players who had been involved in paternity suits included Larry Bird, Patrick Ewing, Juwan Howard, Jason Kidd, Hakeem Olajuwon, Gary Payton, Scottie Pippen, and Isiah Thomas. Other players who are voluntarily supporting their out-of-wedlock children include Kenny Anderson, Allen Iverson, and Latrell Sprewell, the last of whom had three children by three women before he turned twenty-one. Forward Shawn Kemp, who is unmarried, has fathered seven children with six women.

"I'd say there might be more kids out of wedlock [by NBA players] than there are players," according to one of the league's top agents. To Tom Penichter, associate director of Mentors in Violence Prevention, "what [all this] says is a very negative message: those guys are defining for millions of kids growing up what it means to be a successful man."

An earthquake that struck Mexico City in the mid-1980s was less powerful than the one that would hit San Francisco only a few years later. But in Mexico City the casualties were many times higher, and the overall damage much worse. The reason: The amount of devastation often depends less on the magnitude of a quake than on the stability of the structures it affects.

Stars like Madonna and Larry Johnson stand on some very stable structures. They command salaries and resources that few people in the world can match. They can hire whatever help they want. They can send their children to the best schools, provide them with the finest medical care in the world, and meet their every material need. "Their fortunes do somewhat gild their mischiefs, and their purses compound for their follies" is how the seventeenth-century physician and author Sir Thomas Browne described the heedless behavior of the well-to-do.

But Madonna and Larry Johnson are high-profile examples of what is, predominantly, a lower-class phenomenon: illegitimacy. For the *typical* unwed mother—low income, poorly educated, living in America's inner cities—the effects of having children out of wedlock are more often devastating than not. An earthquake that hits a structure already weak and unprotected leaves little standing in its wake.

Whether they like it or not, whether they admit it or not, Madonna, Johnson, and countless other such celebrities and stars are role models for the young. They teach by example, and unfortunately their example is spreading. In word and deed, more and more people have abandoned the forms and the ideals of marriage and parenthood. Some of them do it in the name of freedom, some in the name of convenience, some even in the name of love. Whatever the rationale, the result is that we live in a time when cohabitation without marriage has become standard, when unwed births are at a record level, and when fathers are deserting mothers and children in unprecedented numbers.

Cohabitation, illegitimacy, fatherlessness: In taking up these three topics, I do not mean either to place them in an ascending order of seriousness or to suggest that they are related in a simple, linear fashion. Rather, they follow, roughly, one common pattern of many contemporary lives, in which cohabitation may lead to an illegitimate birth and, in the absence of marital commitment, to an easy exit for the father. (In fact, as we shall see, illegitimacy is closely linked with fatherlessness.) In any case, whether related causally or not, these three phenomena *are* related logically, socially, and culturally, being conjoined instances of the disastrous decline in sexual morality and the wholesale erasure of both inner and outer restraints on self-destructive behavior. Maybe not for the heedless and cushioned Madonna, but for millions upon millions who want to be like her, the consequence of these trends is ever deepening personal unhappiness and social damage that threatens to haunt us for generations.

II

Janna Cordeiro and Stephan Toomey, both in their early thirties, fell in love ten years ago while attending college. Today they live together, having made a firm commitment *not* to make a firm commitment—to marriage, that is. "We didn't want a relationship based on some false sense of security," Cordeiro told *USA Today*. "Our relationship is about getting up and treating each other each day with respect and love. I don't need a marriage license to give me that."

Cordeiro and Toomey are planning on having a baby, but they still resist the idea of marriage. "I am not concerned about any stigma," says Cordeiro. "The most important thing is [that] the child is loved, not whether we have a license."

Thirty-five or forty years ago, living together was not only rare, it was socially taboo. Even decades after Frank Capra had gently spoofed (and honored) the straitlaced conventions of an earlier age in the romantic comedy *It Happened One Night* (1934), parents of young people who were "shacking up" could still hardly bring themselves to acknowledge the fact to their friends or welcome the young couple to their home, and would figuratively tear out their hair in anxiety over the fate of their wayward children. The disapprobation of non- or extramarital sexual relations was reinforced in society by the routine refusal of hotels to admit obviously unmarried couples as guests (forcing the intrepid to sign in under assumed names).

Today, all stigma removed, cohabitation is not only widespread but elicits virtually no public criticism. In 2000, 5.5 million couples cohabited—a more than elevenfold increase from 1960. During the 1990s alone, the number of cohabiting households increased by more than seventy percent. Such households often consist of more than just a couple. About half of previously married cohabitors and thirty-five percent of never-married cohabitors have children with them, and about forty percent of all children born outside of marriage today are born to cohabiting couples. In sum, cohabitation is increasingly seen less as a scandalous prelude to marriage than as a wholly acceptable alternative.

What accounts for the sudden rise in cohabitation? One factor is surely the belief among many people that living together offers many of the benefits of marriage (sex and companionship, to name just two) without its responsibilities and demands. "Why buy the cow when you can get the milk for nothing?" is one common (and vulgar) way of putting it.

Another factor often cited is that the current generation of young Americans is the first to have come of age in a divorce culture. Many of them have seen how fragile marriage is, and this has made them reluctant to enter into a lifelong commitment to another person. The vast majority of adult children of divorced parents, for example, are in favor of cohabiting.

A third explanation has to do with the rise of modern feminism. "Marriage is the mechanism by which the patriarchy is maintained," it was once routinely held, and marriage was also said to encourage domestic abuse. The feminist leader Gloria Steinem declared in 1987 that she was unlikely to marry because in wedlock a woman becomes a "semi-non-person." (Ms. Steinem became a first-time bride last year at the age of sixty-six and declared herself "happy" and "surprised.") Other reasons include the increased acceptance of premarital sex, the greater economic independence of women, and the weakened influence in American life of traditional religious beliefs.

Even for people intending to marry, one great appeal of cohabitation is that it is said to be excellent preparation for the wedded state. According to surveys, most young people think it is a good idea to live together to test compatibility, weed out unsuitable partners, and thereby ensure a long-lasting marriage. The Hollywood actress Susan Sarandon, who has lived for a decade with Tim Robbins, argues that cohabitation helps preserve relationships—"When you say 'till death do us part,' you don't have to reaffirm your love for each other as often"—and hers is hardly an isolated opinion.

But is it right? The evidence suggests otherwise—decisively otherwise. In the case of couples who cohabit before marriage, for example, virtually all research has concluded that contrary to the by-now-longstanding popular wisdom, the chances of a subsequent divorce are significantly *greater*—indeed, almost double—than in the case of couples who marry without prior cohabitation. And when children are involved, the odds of a couple breaking up are higher still.

Does cohabitation help preserve relationships, as Susan Sarandon asserts? Only about one-sixth of couples who cohabit stay together at least three years, and only one-tenth last five years or more. In other words, for most people, these are inherently *un*stable arrangements.

This does not mean, of course, that couples who live together and later marry will inevitably divorce. Nor does it mean that couples who cohabit without marriage cannot live happy and fulfilled lives. Nor does it mean that they cannot raise healthy and productive children. It means, rather, that these things are less likely to happen—*far* less likely to happen—when couples live together than when they marry.

Research tells us other surprising things. In defending single motherhood, some feminists have suggested that the traditional family is itself a breeder of violence against women and other "dysfunctional" behaviors. "One out of every two marriages," claims Libby Bortz, a psychiatric social worker and community activist in Denver, "contains one episode—at least one episode—of physical violence," and "one of every three or four . . . female children under the age of eighteen experiences sexual abuse." The truth is the opposite: What increases the risk of domestic violence against women, plus the risk of physical and sexual abuse of children, is living together *outside* of marriage. Cohabitation also increases the likelihood both of depression and, specifically, of sexual unhappiness: Cohabiting couples show *lower* levels of sexual satisfaction than do married couples.

When couples live together without marriage, it is the women who suffer disproportionately. For example, unmarried couples living together are less likely to pool their joint income, and this hurts women more than men because typically women earn less than men. The inherent instability of the relationship is also more psychologically harmful to women, who not only seek commitment more than men do but also honor it more in practice. According to research compiled by Maggie Gallagher and Linda J. Waite in *The Case for Marriage*, although cohabiting relationships are prone to infidelity on both sides, twice as many cohabiting men as women were unfaithful in a given year. Women often end up with the responsibilities of marriage—particularly when it comes to caring for children—without the legal protection.

And as for those children: Their poverty rate is, on average, five times higher than that of children in married-couple households. Children who come from cohabiting households also perform worse in school, and are more likely to have mental health problems.

In short, far from resembling the cast of a television sitcom like *Friends*, let alone that fantasy of feminist scholarship—the mature, independent couple unhung-up by the power relationships of "traditional" marriage—the typical cohabiting pair make a dreary sight: sexually less satisfied, by a long shot, than their married counterparts; emotionally, ditto; financially much less secure, with little or no prospect of building family wealth; and teetering far more frequently on the edge of breakup.

Why is cohabitation so likely to lead to marital instability? One obvious explanation is circular in nature: People who tend to cohabit are not firmly committed to the institution of marriage in the first place, and are thus quicker to leave a relationship when it hits tough times. But experts tell us that even when they control for this "selection effect," they still find that cohabitation has a negative influence on later marital stability. Indeed, some evidence suggests that the act of cohabiting *itself* may be at fault, perhaps because it inculcates or reinforces attitudes that actively subvert marital permanence: insecurity, infidelity, the desire to escape responsibilities as soon as children are born.

William Doherty, director of the Marriage and Family Therapy Program at the University of Minnesota in Minneapolis, once believed that living together would be a good way for couples to find out if they were compatible marriage partners. Experience has been sobering for him as for many others in this field. Having once believed it was a good idea, he came to regard it as a matter of indifference to society and then, with the passage of still more time, as positively harmful. Doherty attributes his change of mind to an accumulation of factors, including his own research and that of other social scientists into the hurtful effects of cohabitation on future marriages, as well as his growing concern about the erosion of marital commitment in our increasingly throwaway culture.

Proponents of cohabitation often argue that living together "actually looks a good deal like a conventional marriage," as one textbook puts it. But in fact cohabitation is nothing like marriage. Aside from the fact that there is no public ritual or ceremony, no declaration of commitment made before family, friends, and God, people who cohabit also do not acquire relatives and kin, and are therefore denied an important network of support. (For example, if a young couple needs financial help, a father is far less likely to lend money to his daughter's boyfriend than to a son-in-law.) When there are no children involved, which is frequently the case—and frequently the point—the relationship, severed from the rhythms of procreation and generational continuity, is likewise thoroughly detached from the ethos of life in family. And if children *are* involved, they find themselves without grandparents, aunts, uncles, and cousins; their "family tree" has been pruned of many of its branches.

Nor is there a widely accepted "social script" to offer guidance. Unmarried partners must *create* a relationship in ways that married couples do not have to, negotiating everything from how they will arrange their legal affairs to how they will deal with each other's parents to finances to sexual fidelity. On the supremely important matter of children, "the non-parent partner . . . has no explicit legal, financial, supervisory, or custodial rights or responsibilities," writes Linda J. Waite—scriptlessness writ large.

This is, in short, a situation ripe for exploitation, and there is often little doubt as to who is the exploiter, who the exploited. Listen to the all-too-typical testimony of a woman who bought the ideology of cohabitation and lived to regret it:

> I was wrong and I know it. All that stuff about freedom and independence are empty words. . . . It did offer convenience

and freedom all right, but only for [my partner] Jim. . . .
After six months I could realize how this relationship was
putting me deeper into insecurity and exploitation. I was in-
vesting my time and effort looking after him, I was neglect-
ing my career, and had nothing in return, except that I could
leave him at any time, which for me was far from a privilege.

To sum up: Widespread cohabitation delivers, in practice, nothing of what it promises in theory. To the contrary, it undermines
lasting attachments, mutual obligations, successful child-rearing,
and sexual fidelity. It undermines those precious things themselves,
and it undermines our belief in them. What it offers instead is a
kind of institutionalized adolescence: a dream of free love freely be-
stowed, a love relying solely on the springs of mutual emotion and
independent of the legal and other constraints imposed by state
and society and their surrogates in the form of traditional family
arrangements.

It is a pretty enough dream—even if, like many an adolescent
dream, fundamentally irresponsible. The only hitch is that in actual
experience it has led directly to injury upon injury upon injury.

Do we care? From the proponents of cohabitation we hear that
the state has no business interfering in people's private lives, no business curtailing their freedom of personal action or regulating their
domestic arrangements. The answer, which cannot be repeated often
enough, is that the state has a manifest interest in promoting the
kind of stability that rests on sound marriages and strong families.
And so does each one of us. To the extent that cohabitation becomes
a replacement for marriage, we are all worse off. That so many people now think otherwise merely illustrates how much ground has
been lost in our understanding of the purposes of family life. That
so many people *act* otherwise is a measure of how much needs to be
recovered, and how many wasted lives cry out for rescue.

III

Here is one of the most stunning facts of our time: *One-third of all births are to unmarried women.* Among whites, the proportion of out-of-wedlock births to all births was 2.3 percent in 1960; it is 26.7 percent today. Among blacks, the number increased from over twenty percent in 1960 to almost seventy percent today, a figure, writes Charles Murray, "unprecedented for any large subpopulation of any culture, ancient or modern."

The figures are even more stunning when we look at the most emotionally vulnerable cohort: unmarried *teen* mothers, who account for almost a third of all nonmarital births. Over seventy percent of white teenage mothers are unmarried. For Latina teen mothers, the figure is seventy-three percent. And for black teen mothers, the figure is a staggering ninety-six percent. In this important segment of the maternal population, marriage is virtually a forgotten institution.

During the decade of the 1990s, we made progress on a whole range of social issues, crime and welfare most prominently among them. Not this one: The illegitimacy problem *worsened* in the '90s, with the percentage of nonmarital births rising in all age groups, in small towns and large cities, in all regions and states, in all socioeconomic groups.

But not evenly across all groups: far from it. Women who have children out of wedlock tend to be poor, young, less educated, and with fewer career opportunities—not, in short, Madonna. According to census data, women with incomes under $20,000 are responsible for almost three-quarters of all illegitimate births, and more than half who give birth as teenagers show a total family income well below the poverty line. An unmarried woman without a high school diploma is at least three times as likely to have a child as an unmarried woman who has attended college.

What this means is that illegitimacy is largely a class phenomenon. In many upper-income communities, you will find very few unwed mothers. In poor, inner-city communities, by contrast, the overwhelming percentage of births are to unwed single women who are the least able economically to care for children. These women are often forced to go on welfare or to get by on menial jobs, and their chances of improving themselves are bleak. Abandoned by their men, they have been abandoned no less cruelly by the American Left, by the enthusiastic advocates of female sexual "liberation," and by the noisy critics of a "patriarchy" from which, in a benevolent form, they could only stand to benefit.

Nor does the harm stop with the mothers themselves. Illegitimacy is a major killer of American children. Surveying over two hundred thousand children born in Georgia, the Centers for Disease Control concluded that birth certificates lacking a father's name were strong predictors of infant death. According to the demographer Nicholas Eberstadt: "If it were a medical condition rather than a social syndrome, illegitimacy would have been ranked the third or fourth leading cause of death for infants in America."

Even when they survive infancy, children born out of wedlock are more likely, and in many instances *far* more likely, to die young, to live in poverty, to be on welfare, to perpetuate a crime, to commit suicide, to drop out of the labor force, to leave school, and to have illegitimate children themselves. Seventy percent of America's adolescent murderers, and of America's long-term prisoners, come from fatherless homes.

These are just some of the things the illegitimacy revolution has wrought. And yet public attitudes on this issue, especially among women, have so far refused to confront reality. More than sixty percent of young women aged eighteen to twenty-four, for example, agree with the statement that "one parent can bring up a child as well as two parents." Similarly, the proportion of female high school seniors who think that having a child without being married is a worthy "lifestyle," or does not affect anyone else, has sharply increased during the last two decades.

Gone for good, it seems, is the very concept of bastardy—and few may lament its passing. But in the meantime, those who point to the evidence of widespread and deep social suffering as a result of what was once called bastardy are typically dismissed as cranks. To express concern about out-of-wedlock births is, in the words of one liberal writer, to adopt "*The Scarlet Letter* as a primer on what to do about illegitimacy." Or it is said to be an exercise in "heaping scorn" on unwed mothers, an exercise rooted in censoriousness, or even misogyny. The late syndicated columnist Carl Rowan accused public figures who speak out against unmarried births of spreading "subtle demagogic racism."

Is there any truth in these charges? In some cases, there may be. But can one also make a principled case against illegitimacy? Yes, assuredly. Though the illegitimacy rate is higher in the black community, the majority of unmarried mothers in America are white, a fact that makes the racism charge itself demagogic as well as flatly untrue. As for misogyny, having a child out of wedlock is, as we have seen, one of the *worst* things that can happen to a woman in terms of economic circumstances and future prospects. Is it being antiwoman to say so? Hardly.

Clearly, it is in the area of attitudes, of moral sentiments, that the matter of illegitimacy will ultimately be settled. Until it is, and no matter how bravely they try to convince themselves to the contrary, young women will go on suffering the horrid consequences of this epidemic; and so will their children, and so will the rest of us. Only Madonna and her like will escape scot-free.

IV

Having pointed out that the majority of unmarried mothers in the United States are white, let me now say a word about the special case of illegitimacy in the black community, where the *rates* of illegitimacy are much, much higher. My reference point is a 1965 study entitled "The Negro Family: The Case for National Action." This, the so-called Moynihan Report, is one of the most important pieces of social science ever produced, and reverting to it will help us understand the magnitude of the crisis that now engulfs us.

"The Negro Family" was written in the heady days following the passage of the great Civil Rights Act of 1964, when the demand for legal equality for American blacks was finally met. Its author was Daniel Patrick Moynihan, then an assistant secretary of labor in the Johnson administration and later to become a distinguished American senator. The report stated flatly that "the single most important social fact in the United States" was the breakup of the black family.

Today, the deteriorating condition of the black family is a well-known and much-commented-upon topic. Not so in the mid-1960s. So sensitive was the subject then that, according to the reporters Rowland Evans and Robert Novak, attempts were actually made to suppress Moynihan's study. Once it did become public, it was bitterly attacked by some for encouraging "subtle racism." Moynihan himself endured harsh personal abuse for having raised, however thoughtfully, a topic deemed too controversial to be addressed.

For our purposes, over thirty-five years later, the Moynihan Report raises two different considerations. One is the amount of ground the nation has *lost* over the last three and a half decades. The other is the degree to which we have become inured to the trauma.

Among both rural and urban blacks, the rate of cohabitation had always been rather high; but those cohabiting tended to be older rather than younger, and if the woman became pregnant, marriage was the rule rather than the exception. What Moynihan noticed in 1965 was a jump in the rate not of black cohabitation but of illegitimacy. By that year, one-quarter of all black children were being born out of wedlock. A little more than half of all black children lived in broken homes at some time before they reached the age of eighteen. Nearly a quarter of all black women who had married were living apart from their husbands. Fourteen percent of black children were on welfare. Faced with this "tangle of pathologies," Moynihan wrote: "There is a considerable body of evidence to support the conclusion that Negro social structure, in particular the Negro family . . . is in the deepest trouble."

When the Moynihan Report was finally made public, *Newsweek* called its numbers "stunning." Even a prominent critic of Moynihan like William Ryan of Harvard warned of the "frightening statistics" it presented about "broken Negro families, illegitimate Negro children, and Negro welfare recipients." Martin Luther King, Jr., declared the breakdown of the Negro family a "social catastrophe."

These comments were made, remember, when "only" one-quarter of black children were born to unwed mothers. Today, almost *seventy percent* of black children are born to unwed mothers. Nearly eighty percent of black women will be the head of the family at some point in their childbearing years, and of black children born in 1980, the projections are that more than eighty percent will have been dependent on welfare at one point or another during childhood. As a nation, we would surely give our collective eyeteeth to be back in the "frightening" situation of 1965.

For if that situation represented a "social catastrophe"—as indeed it did—what words can possibly describe our situation today? The Moynihan Report, remember, had little to say about the *white* family, apart from noting that it had "achieved a high degree of stability and is maintaining that stability." During the intervening thirty-five years, white family structure has likewise severely eroded, with illegitimacy alone leaping from four to twenty-five percent. So in this as in so much else, we are all, black and white, in this together.

Social catastrophe? More like a cataclysm. But few indeed are those willing to admit to the reality, let alone willing to address what might be done about it.

V

A woman with a child, it has been said, is a natural fact; a man with a child is a social achievement. What this means is that a mother's devotion to her infant child is, for a host of reasons, deeper and more reliable than a father's. "Compared to mothers," David Blankenhorn writes, "fathers are less born than made. As a social role, fatherhood is less the inelastic result of sexual embodiment than the fragile creation of cultural norms."

A fragile creation, perhaps, but also an imperative one. The anthropologist Bronislaw Malinowski believed in a universal sociological law that he called "the principle of legitimacy." According to Malinowski:

> The most important moral and legal rule concerning the physiological side of kinship is that no child should be brought into the world without a man—and one man at that—assuming the role of sociological father, that is, of guardian and protector, the male link between the child and the rest of the community.

True, the principle of legitimacy assumes different forms in different cultures. But "through all these variations," Malinowski wrote, "there runs the rule that the father is indispensable for the full sociological status of the child as well as of its mother, that the group consisting of a woman and her offspring is sociologically incomplete and illegitimate. The father, in other words, is necessary for the full legal status of the family."

Throughout history, every human society has recognized this "principle of legitimacy." No longer. We twenty-first-century moderns have set sail upon uncharted social waters. Not only is fatherlessness "now approaching a rough parity with fatherhood as a defining feature of American childhood," in David Blankenhorn's words, but *attitudes* toward fatherlessness have undergone a radical shift as well. Today, in many quarters, the idea that a child needs a father is viewed as quaint, even pre-modern. Fathers are great if you can get them, but by no means irreplaceable. Other men—even no men—will do just fine.

The father-as-appendage idea is everywhere. It is voiced by the likes of the movie actress and popular talk show host Rosie O'Donnell, herself a single mother (through adoption) of three children. When asked about the "father" question, she says she tells her children that "all families are different, and that we don't have a daddy. That works for them. They have a very clear understanding about who the people are in their family, and they . . . have very strong male influences. My brothers are around frequently, as is my [male] friend."

A more scholarly version of this same attitude appears in a recent article, "Deconstructing the Essential Father," in *American Psychologist,* a magazine sent to almost every practicing psychologist in America. According to the authors, Louise Silverstein and Carl Auerbach, a father makes no "unique and essential" contribution to his child's development, and other "responsible, caretaking" adults can do the task just as well. Not only can "emotionally connected, actively nurturing, and responsible fathering . . . occur within a variety of family structures," the very effort to strengthen the old mother-father idea of marriage is itself pernicious: an attempt to reassert "the cultural hegemony of traditional values, such as heterocentrism, Judeo-Christian marriage, and male power and privilege."

In untangling this unholy mess, perhaps the place to start is with the claim that all kinds of family structures can do equally well by children. In the words of Silverstein and Auerbach: "Our research with divorced, never-married, and remarried fathers has taught us that a wide variety of family structures can support positive child outcomes."

Note the use of "can." It is, of course, *possible* for a never-married parent to raise healthy, well-adjusted, well-educated children. But the implication that children of "divorced, never-married, and remarried" parents do as well *on average* as children raised by two married parents is utterly false. The data support what common sense tells us: There is no "alternative family structure" that is nearly as good for a child as a family that includes a married mother and father.

We may also question whether "male friends" and other "responsible caretakers" can be counted on in most instances to demonstrate the devotion to and love for a child that we expect of a father. That proposition would be questionable even if there were enough friends and "caretakers" to go around, which there are not. I say this as someone who was raised by a mother and grandmother, without a father at home, and who is deeply indebted to the many good men who guided me. Even so, I know that other men, even other very good men, are imperfect substitutes: For most children, the early, consistent presence of a father is irreplaceable.

In this connection, let me tie together two fascinating bits of social science data. The first is that children with stepfathers demonstrate almost as many behavioral problems as children in single-parent families. Thus, according to an in-depth study of one Canadian city, children under the age of five living with a natural parent and a stepparent are *forty* times more likely to be the victims of abuse than are children living with two natural parents. This is so despite the fact that many stepfathers are fine people who genuinely care for their stepchildren.

The second is that children whose fathers have died fare considerably *better* than children who gain a stepfather via divorce and remarriage. Why? The most compelling explanation I have heard is that children whose fathers die—particularly in war, or in the line of duty—retain a positive, even idealized view of a man whose memory is revered and whose moral authority endures. This is a function of the mother's memory as well as the child's. By contrast, a father who leaves his children also leaves behind feelings of abandonment and resentment.

Not nearly enough fathers are meeting their commitments to their children; this we know. Is that a reason to devalue fatherhood even more, or should we, instead, try to shore up a cultural norm that has been wantonly debased? And if it is to be the latter, as I believe it must, how shall we go about the task?

We can start by reminding ourselves of the fundamental meaning, and responsibilities, of a father.

Whether he wants to or not, a father provides his children with a model of how to live—including an example of how a husband ought to treat his wife. The details of the model may vary from particular family to particular family. Some women excel at traditional male responsibilities, and the opposite is true as well. And there is, of course, tremendous overlap in what fathers and mothers provide. Nor do the "manly virtues" preclude paternal affection, emotional accessibility, tenderness. But in general, as I have already had occasion to note, men and women bring different, complementary traits to child-rearing, and these differences, I firmly believe, are not mere social constructions but are rooted in biology and the natural order of things—"certain old truths which will be true as long as this world endures," as Theodore Roosevelt once wrote.

The time-honored responsibility of fathers is to protect their children from the world—and to protect the world from their children. Most fathers are sources of discipline and strength, respect and admiration: embodiments of what we once called, without embarrassment, the manly virtues. A father enforces boundaries, teaches the importance of self-restraint and duty, provides physical safety and, for many families, both financial security and spiritual guidance. Indeed, one of the things that can most profoundly shape a child's early understanding of God the Father—who, we are told in the Book of Exodus, is "compassionate and gracious, slow to anger, abounding in love and faithfulness"—is the degree to which that child feels loved and nurtured by his earthly father: a reminder to all of us of the work we are called upon to do.

Any parent knows that raising a child is an experience filled with wonder and exhilaration, and any parent also knows that it is hard work—harder, often, when it comes to young boys than to young girls. For young boys in particular are inclined toward antisocial behavior, and their passions need to be checked, tamed, and channeled. This is a job for which fathers are preeminently qualified. (I would only add here that daughters need their fathers—their earliest, most enduring, and most consequential image of manhood—just as much. Daughters abandoned by their fathers early in life are often profoundly affected for the worse in terms of future relationships with men.)

What happens when the male template shatters, and boys grow up with no tangible, living example of what it means to be a responsible man, a faithful husband, a good father, a good citizen? Often they become sexual predators, chronically violent, unruly, angry, uncontrolled. Street corners resemble scenes from *Lord of the Flies* or *Fight Club*. This is not mere speculation; and it is, by the way, true among other species besides the human, as the following story illustrates.

Kruger National Park is South Africa's largest conservation area. Twenty years ago, when it had many more elephants than the park could sustain, researchers decided to kill off some of the adults and relocate some of the easily transportable children. These younger elephants were eventually resettled in Pilanesberg National Park.

All seemed well until, a few years later, Pilanesberg began to experience the unexplained slaughter of its white rhinos. Although the obvious explanation was poachers, this turned out not to be the case. When park rangers set up hidden video cameras, they discovered that young, hyperaggressive bull elephants were harassing the rhinos, chasing them over long distances, and, finally, goring them to death with their tusks.

This was extremely puzzling; elephants, after all, are generally docile creatures and rarely, if ever, attack other animals. But it turned out that these "orphaned" elephants had developed into a band of marauding teenagers, led by "gang leaders." Normally, older bull elephants function as a civilizing presence to keep the young males in line—but these transplanted elephants, according to Gus van Dyk, the Pilanesberg field ecologist, "had no role model and no idea of what appropriate elephant behavior was."

The solution was to transport to Pilanesberg some older, mature bulls, creating, in the words of CBS correspondent Bob Simon, "the biggest Big Brother program in the world." Within weeks, discipline was established and the younger elephants began to follow the older bull elephants around, imitating them and exhibiting "good" behavior, and even seeming to enjoy the presence of their elder role models. Since the experiment began, there have been no reports of killed rhinos.

Can our society survive the equivalent of many Pilanesberg game preserves *before* the arrival of mature bull elephants? Up to a point, it can. But doing so requires a massive police presence and a high incarceration rate as, in the absence of fathers, law enforcement officers and prisons step in to control our unsocialized young men. The United States already has the highest incarceration rate in the world, with more than two million persons in federal and state prisons and local jails (in 1980, the figure was just over 500,000). Today we deploy almost three-quarters of a million full-time, sworn law enforcement officers, and Americans spend more than $15 billion annually on personal security systems.

This ought to be deeply alarming. As with cohabitation, it is often said these days that the private sexual behavior of two people is of no legitimate interest to the wider community, and if a couple has a child out of wedlock, that is nobody's business but their own. Clearly, that is not so. Illegitimacy and fatherlessness have costly consequences, being linked, as we have seen, to infant mortality, crime, joblessness, homelessness, educational failure, and the disintegration of whole neighborhoods.

To the degree that out-of-wedlock births elicit any criticism these days, most of it is directed toward the women who bear these children. But remember: In almost every instance, a single woman will not abandon her illegitimate child. Although there are, certainly, men who father children out of wedlock and want to do the right thing but are prevented (often when the mother has a new boyfriend), they are exceptions to the rule. In general, it is unmarried fathers who are missing in record numbers, who impregnate women and selfishly flee. And it is these absent men, above all, who deserve our censure and disesteem. Abandoning alike those whom they have taken as sexual partners and those whose lives they have created, they strike at the heart of the marital ideal, traduce generations yet to come, and disgrace their very manhood.

VI

How did all this come to pass? In 1994, Kay Hymowitz, a contributing editor at *City Journal,* spent some time in the inner-city neighborhoods of New York interviewing young single mothers. What she discovered was "a culture—or subculture to be precise—with its own values, beliefs, sexual mores, and, to a certain extent, its own economy . . . a never-never land almost completely abandoned by fathers and, in some sad cases, by mothers as well."

Christie, a sixteen-year-old Latina girl, told Hymowitz that her first sexual encounter had taken place two years earlier, because she was "sick of being the only fourteen-year-old virgin around." Fourteen-year-old Taisha Brown said: "My mother already told me, 'If you get pregnant, you won't have an abortion. You'll have the baby, and your grandmother and I will help out.' " When asked about a father, she answered: "Why do I need to worry about a father? My mother raised me and my sister just fine without one."

Social scientists cite a whole host of reasons for today's epidemic of illegitimacy and fatherlessness: changing sexual mores, an inner-city ethos that values unmarried motherhood more than career achievement, the loss of stigma associated with out-of-wedlock births, a sense of hopelessness in the urban underclass. I submit that another important factor is welfare.

It was once argued that welfare had virtually no effect on illegitimacy. Today, the view among many scholars is that a consequential relationship does exist. This is what I would call an elaborate demonstration of the obvious. The truth is that for decades we have had in place a welfare system that has deliberately *subsidized* out-of-wedlock births. The program called Aid to Families with Dependent Children (AFDC), which began in the 1930s to help "widows and orphans," was transmuted over the decades into a vast government system that in effect has paid poor, unmarried women to have children. Whatever its good intentions, it ranks among the most destructive social initiatives ever.

But, you may ask, what about the 1996 welfare reform bill, the Personal Responsibility and Work Opportunity Reconciliation Act? Has not that had a positive effect on the behavior of welfare recipients? It is a good question. This enormously significant legislation represented the first-ever repeal of a federal entitlement, replacing AFDC with something called Temporary Assistance to Needy Families (TANF). Allowing greater flexibility to states than in the past, TANF also made it easier to incorporate rigorous new work requirements and performance standards for welfare recipients.

The results have indeed been stunning: Since 1994 (the peak year), welfare rolls have been cut in half. True, there is some debate over the exact role played by certain ongoing reforms in individual states that the welfare bill may have merely ratified, and also over how much credit for the drop goes to the booming economy of the late 1990s and/or increases in aid to the working poor (for example, in the form of the Earned Income Tax Credit). Still, there is no question but that welfare reform is responsible for a large percentage of the total decline in welfare rolls and must be considered one of the most successful social policies of the last half-century.

But it affects *work,* not illegitimacy. And on the latter, the news is disheartening. During the same period when welfare rolls were being reduced by fifty percent, the percentage of births out of wedlock was growing. And of the five states that saw the greatest decrease in welfare between 1994 and 1997, four saw an increase in the out-of-wedlock birth ratio.

Obviously, having people work is far better than not, and a job can provide a stability that is badly needed, particularly in the inner cities of America. But the major problem confronting American society is not the large numbers of single mothers without jobs; it is, rather, the large numbers of unmarried women who are having babies. What can be done about *that?*

I myself would not be as quick as some are to give up on targeted programs of welfare reform. Of course, defenders of the status quo argue that welfare is not the problem in the first place. It is absurd, they say, to think a woman would bear a child in order to collect a cash payment. For that would suggest that "these girls are on some level planning their pregnancies," says Kristin A. Moore, executive director of Child Trends, Inc., and "study after study shows that they don't."

This misses the point. Even apart from the fact that an assortment of noncash benefits (housing, food stamps, Medicaid) is far more valuable than cash payments, what welfare has done is to make illegitimacy economically viable. From the dawn of civilization until the mid-1960s, having a child out of wedlock meant devastating economic hardship to be avoided at almost all costs. No longer.

Bill Clinton made this point well. "I once polled one hundred children in an alternative school in Atlanta—many of whom had had babies out of wedlock," the then president said in an interview with NBC's Tom Brokaw. " 'If we didn't give any [welfare] to people after they had their first child, how many of you think it would reduce the number of out-of-wedlock births?' Over eighty percent of the kids raised their hands."

Here is another relevant fact. The majority of out-of-wedlock births are to women who, a year prior to giving birth, lived below the poverty line. Why would such births be so heavily concentrated among the poor? As the social scientist Charles Murray has written, the sexual revolution may have changed the behavior of young women at all levels of society, but it has produced babies in predominantly just one economic class: the poor. A reasonable person could well conclude, with University of Pennsylvania Professor Elijah Anderson, that "in cold economic terms, a baby can be an asset." Perhaps, then, welfare does have a significant negative effect on the unmarried birth ratio.

What then? Some people believe that even so, there is no alternative to the present system: You cannot simply cut off benefits to unwed mothers without causing a social calamity. So deeply ingrained is the illegitimacy ethic among the urban underclass that no policy can undo it. Well, the truth is that neither the advocates nor the critics of ending subsidies for illegitimacy can say with absolute confidence what the effects would be. The only way to prove who is right and who is wrong is to test.

I am also skeptical of the idea that we must stick to inherently flawed policies because we lack confidence in people's capacity to change. Nor do I think it is wise to enshrine illegitimacy incentives in law. As it now stands, these laws produce two nearly inevitable consequences: births to unwed women and a reinforcement of the idea that having children out of wedlock is a fine thing. Even former Secretary of Health and Human Services Donna Shalala, of impeccable liberal credentials, has said: "I don't like to put this in moral terms, but I do believe that having children out of wedlock is just wrong."

But, critics of welfare reform might counter finally, what about the children involved—who are, after all, innocent parties? The goal of reform may be to deny benefits to the mother, but the result will be that they end up hurting the child. In response, I would point again to the calamitous things that are happening under the current welfare regime. Since we began subsidizing out-of-wedlock births in the 1960s, the federal government has compiled an astonishingly brutal record, details of which I have given in the earlier sections of this chapter. And the ratio continues its relentless march upward—meaning that things have to change if we are to avoid even greater social ruin. The burden of proof ought to rest not on those who would try something new, but on those who support policies that have helped to destroy large parts of an entire generation.

What we might hope to see within the next few years is a state, or several states, willing to begin the work of uprooting a system that continues to foster illegitimacy and its attendant social maladies. The state cannot compel people to marry. But the benefit of letting states try different approaches is that we can see which works best.

One such approach is to promote a culture of marriage. An example can be found in Oklahoma, where Governor Frank Keating has set aside $10 million in TANF funds to encourage marriage, reduce out-of-wedlock pregnancies, and foster the formation and maintenance of two-parent families. Some of the specific actions include working with religious leaders to help develop community-based, marriage-strengthening programs; training workers to teach marriage skills courses; and documenting state divorce trends. To his credit, Governor Keating has set a goal of reducing the state's divorce rate by one-third by 2010.

But there is more that can be done. My own hope is that at least one state will pass legislation cutting off future benefits to a particular subset of the population (say, unmarried teen mothers) while also actively expanding group homes for pregnant single women; promoting adoption; and enforcing already existing laws that allow the state to protect neglected and abused children. Other states might target other subsets of the population. Let me underscore a crucial point, however: It is only fair, and wise, to "grandfather" those now in the system, allowing them to retain the benefit package they receive under existing rules. Thus, to take a hypothetical example, if a never-married mother has five children, her existing benefits would not be reduced if she had a sixth. But, one year after legislation was passed, she would receive no *new* support.

I have said previously that unwed fathers are most deserving of our disesteem. Why, then, am I advocating public policies targeted mainly at women? There is, unfortunately, little help for it. For one thing, eighty-seven percent of adult AFDC recipients in 1994 were female—which only underlines the problem of selfish, irresponsible men. It has been suggested that for men who have been imprisoned, we might link time on parole to responsible sexual behavior. But this would be a tricky thing to enforce. In the end, I think, we have to admit that our leverage with men is limited. What we can hope is that if women's behavior changes, men's will too. History and everyday experience give us reason to think this hope is not misplaced.*

I am under no illusions. Breaking the cycle of illegitimacy ultimately depends on stopping widespread, deeply entrenched, highly destructive behavior. In inner cities all across America, the vast majority of children are born without fathers in their lives; to restore the two-parent norm in these communities—to say nothing of the rest of the nation—is a monumental undertaking. Compounding the problem are the powerful cultural forces, from the assault on "patriarchy" and "traditional values" to the celebration of single motherhood, from the taboo on "judgmentalism" to the ethic of entitlement, that rationalize the phenomenon of illegitimacy not just in the United States but throughout most of the Western world.

And yet there are few more important social challenges. Policy

---

* Programs that encourage abstinence, such as the program Best Friends, proceed from just this assumption. And they are successful.

reforms may not be sufficient to the task, but they are necessary. Moreover, they send an important signal about what we Americans are willing to affirm and what we are prepared to repudiate. Terrible human wreckage has been left in illegitimacy's wake. We need to ask ourselves whether we are prepared to do anything about it, and we need to ask ourselves, and answer ourselves, soon.

Homosexual Unions

I

Forty years ago, in the novel and then the movie *Advise and Consent,* a young congressman is discovered to be homosexual and commits suicide. Four years ago, in April 1997, the title character on ABC's sitcom *Ellen* announced she was a lesbian, to rather different effect.

At about the time news of the impending program was first released, the show's star, Ellen DeGeneres, declared that like the character she played, she herself was homosexual. These twin revelations created, in the words of *Time* magazine, "a minor national obsession," attracting a huge amount of coverage, almost all of which was sympathetic. Across the United States, enthusiastic viewers held "welcome out" parties in homes, bars, and civic centers. "We are just going to whoop it up," Joseph Pouliot, a gay college sophomore in Washington, D.C., told *USA Today*. Elizabeth Birch, executive director of Human Rights Campaign, the largest political lobby for gay issues, hailed this episode of *Ellen* as a "monumental move" in American popular culture. "America has never quite seen anything like this," said Birch, "where the girl next door comes out."

Forty-two million Americans tuned in to watch the episode, which was itself widely praised by critics for its "courage." Six months after the program aired, in a speech to the Hollywood Radio and Television Society, then Vice President Al Gore singled out *Ellen* for its contribution to society. He praised Oscar the Grouch (a puppet character on *Sesame Street*) for teaching children valuable lessons and Archie Bunker (the lead character in *All in the Family*) for forcing Americans to confront their racial and ethnic prejudices. "And," the vice president concluded, "when the character Ellen came out, millions of Americans were forced to look at sexual orientation in a more open light."

If the "coming out" of Ellen was a first for prime-time television, things have since moved very fast. A scant three and a half years later, in December 2000, the cable network Showtime began airing a new drama series, *Queer as Folk*, based on a popular British miniseries and featuring the lives of five young homosexual men and a lesbian couple. Described as an "edgy" and "groundbreaking" new program, *Queer as Folk* lived up to its advance billing. Here is a scene from its opening episode as described by Barbara Phillips in the *Wall Street Journal*:

> They all know that Brian is a heartbreaker, and when a sexually inexperienced, blond, and handsome seventeen-year-old, Justin, turns up in the opening minutes of the series, it is Brian who takes the fresh-faced preppie home to his brick-and-steel loft and introduces him to anal and oral sex. (He attempts to introduce him to drugs, too, but is rebuffed.) After their encounter, Justin thinks he's in love. But Brian has trouble even remembering the boy's name. Heck, Brian is so wasted on illicit substances he can't remember that he

just became a father [via a lesbian who had been insemi-
nated with his sperm].

According to Caryn James of *The New York Times*, the purpose
of *Queer as Folk* was to "reverse society's heterosexual assumptions."
And in that respect, testified Tom Shales, *The Washington Post's* media critic, it got off to a "triumphantly provocative start."

Last year, the Boston chapter of the Gay, Lesbian & Straight Education Network (GLSEN), a national organization sponsored in part
by American Airlines, Dockers Khakis, and Kodak, and under contract in Massachusetts to run educator-training sessions, hosted a
conference at Tufts University near Boston. One of the workshops,
for "youth only, ages fourteen to twenty-one," was called "What
They Didn't Tell You About Queer Sex and Sexuality in Health
Class."

A grassroots organization of alarmed citizens called the Parents'
Rights Coalition (PRC) taped the sessions and then provided the tape
to the media. As recounted by Rod Dreher in the *Weekly Standard*,
the sessions were led by two employees of the Massachusetts Department of Education and an AIDS educator from the Massachusetts
public health agency named Michael Gaucher. One of these sessions,
attended by thirty students, some as young as fourteen, included a
detailed discussion of specific, unusual, and grotesque sexual acts.
The young participants were urged to consult with their Gay/
Straight Alliance adviser for tips on how to "come on" to a potential
sex partner.

The transcribed tape, which contained a great deal more along
these lines, was then published in the monthly *Massachusetts News*,
and copies were sent to local radio stations. A storm of controversy
ensued, as a result of which the state's education commissioner fired

one of its two employees, accepted the resignation of the second, and terminated Mr. Gaucher's contract. But the commissioner also defended GLSEN's work in the state schools, terming the incident at Tufts an aberration.

To this, Julie Abels, one of the employees of the Massachusetts Department of Education who participated in the workshop, angrily responded that the department had known all along what she had been doing and had never raised an objection until after the tapes were broadcast. Similarly, the executive director of the AIDS Action Committee protested that firing the two employees would send a chilling message to educators. "These kids were there to learn. You could debate mistakes made in the presentation. But what they did was not wrong."

And the parents who made the tape? They became the objects of public vilification—and of lawsuits. *The Boston Globe* warned against efforts to "inflame" intolerance, while a group called Gay & Lesbian Advocates & Defenders filed a legal action on behalf of the workshop students, threatening to press criminal charges for recording the session secretly. The chairman of the governor's Commission on Gay and Lesbian Youth raised a public alarm over "the prejudice that simmers beneath the surface [which] has now bubbled up into the open in all of its ugliness."

As a result of all the adverse publicity, the co-chair of the Parents' Rights Coalition found his software business suffering. "I could lose everything," he said. "My business could go down the tubes. And if this criminal stuff actually goes down, I could go to jail."

Do the media imitate life, or is it the other way around? That is only one of the questions raised by anecdotes like these, and not the most important one. The root fact to which the media, like the rest of us, are responding is that over the last two decades the "gay rights" agenda has made more headway than perhaps any other political movement in America. Although homosexuals comprise no more than four percent of the population, they boast a plethora of vocal organizations that run the gamut from relatively moderate to very extreme, from the Human Rights Campaign, the Gay and Lesbian Alliance Against Defamation (GLAAD), and the National Gay and Lesbian Task Force (NGLTF) to the AIDS Coalition to Unleash Power (ACT-UP, "united in anger and committed to direct action") and the North American Man/Boy Love Association (NAMBLA, whose openly stated goal is "to end the extreme oppression of men and boys in mutually consensual relationships"). Gay rights activists hold influential, culture-shaping jobs in the literary world, the advertising industry, television and the movies, and have allies in Hollywood and prestigious media outlets like *The New York Times*, *Time, Newsweek,* and the entertainment magazines. With skill, talent, money, and a shrewd sense of tactics, they are articulate advocates for their cause.

That cause has changed substantially with the passage of the years. Once upon a time, proponents of homosexual rights concentrated their efforts on achieving public tolerance and ensuring equality before the law. Homosexuals wanted to be able to go about their lives in society without being the objects of harassment or civil discrimination. But in the last few years, with the growth of the "movement," the goal has become more aggressive: social *approval* and legal *endorsement.* It has become a movement seeking privilege and preferences. This new and far more ambitious project has led to an effort to inculcate in the young the idea that homosexuality and heterosexuality are equally "normal" and equally valid "lifestyles," and, especially, to reshape fundamentally our understanding of marriage and family life. Indeed, for many homosexual activists, the most important goal of the gay rights movement today—and the one on which I shall have the most to say in this chapter—is to gain legal recognition of homosexual marriages.

This more ambitious project has succeeded to a remarkable extent. Moral criticism of homosexuality is today widely considered to be the equivalent of racism. Those who argue that marriage ought to be the exclusive preserve of a man and a woman, or who believe that homosexual adoption is not in the best interest of children, or who do not want their own children to be exposed to courses sympathetic to homosexuality, or who maintain moral objections to homosexual conduct are now routinely portrayed as bigoted, ignorant, and "homophobic." So much headway has this campaign made in the world of opinion that many middle-class Americans who oppose the homosexual agenda often hesitate to say so, and some even do not allow themselves to think so, lest they appear "intolerant." A kind of political correctness reigns, covering the issue of homosexuality with a protective veil of polite silence, if not yet full acquiescence.

From books for elementary-school children like *Heather Has Two Mommies* and *Daddy's Roommate,* to the exhibit by a federally subsidized organization of graphic homosexual photographs by the artist Robert Mapplethorpe, to agitation against the Boy Scouts of America over its standards of membership and leadership, to pressure for the official inclusion of homosexuals in New York's St. Patrick's Day parade, to the flood of gay-themed movies, television programs, and plays, a concerted effort has been under way to present the homosexual "lifestyle" as normal, worthy of public support, and fully equivalent (if not actually superior) to heterosexual marriage and family life. Even the toll taken on the homosexual community by the sexually transmitted disease AIDS has been portrayed as a sign of that community's special status, its roster of martyrs demanding like so many war dead to be publicly mourned in quilts, ribbons, photographic displays, and ritualized invocations of heroism and struggle.

To all this, the American people have responded with a remarkable degree of tolerance—but also, when they are asked, with a firm demurral. As the sociologist Alan Wolfe documents in his book *One Nation, After All*, although a large majority of Americans believe that, for example, homosexuals should be permitted to teach in colleges and universities (an issue of rights), and many also hold that homosexuals can do "whatever they want behind closed doors" (an issue of privacy), still, as many as "seventy percent of the American people believe that sexual relations between members of the same sex is wrong," and there is a distinct tilt against the proposition that "respect for gay lifestyles" should be taught in the public schools.

Instinctively, it would seem, many Americans have grasped a point that eludes the advocates of gay rights: that one can be tolerant of others while declining to accept what they do as right, or as entitling them to public endorsement. At the end of this chapter, I comment on the disfigurement of the idea of tolerance at the hands of the agenda-pushers of our day. Here let me just register my unshakable conviction that it is not wrong—to the contrary, it is highly praiseworthy—to stand up against the campaign of intimidation that would brand as bigots those of us who exercise our elementary responsibility, as parents and as citizens, to make firm moral judgments in matters touching on marriage and the raising of our children.

II

In December 1999, the homosexual rights movement won a landmark victory: The Supreme Court of the state of Vermont ordered the state's legislature either to legalize gay marriage outright or to create some other way of treating same-sex couples as the functional equivalents of married men and women. Faced with this either/or choice, the legislature adopted the somewhat safer of the two routes, passing a "civil union" law that was duly signed by Howard Dean, Vermont's Democratic governor. Under this law, gay partners may apply for a license from a town clerk and get their civil union certified by a justice of the peace, a judge, or a clergyman; partners seeking to dissolve such a union must go through a family court.

The bill allows partners in a civil union to receive virtually the same state benefits as married couples, benefits extending to such matters as hospital visits, inheritance rights, and the transfer of property. Although the word "marriage" is not mentioned, being still reserved for the union of a man and a woman, in Vermont this has in many ways become a distinction without a difference. Virtually all of the arguments made on behalf of civil unions, if taken seriously, *could* have led proponents in the state legislature to legalize same-sex marriage, and clearly *would* have led them to that end had they dared to press the issue to its logical conclusion.

Indeed, the resolution of the Vermont case has created a unique problem for those Americans who think of themselves as allies of the gay rights movement but who would continue to deny homosexual couples the right to marry. Such liberals and "progressives," who have embraced all or most of the movement's positions—on, for example, the right of gays to adopt children, to serve in the military, to lead Boy Scout troops, and to be granted special protection under "hate crimes" legislation—have stopped short of endorsing the idea of gay marriage. But they can offer no morally or legally coherent argument as to *why*.

The opinion of the Vermont court itself, as well as the action subsequently taken by the legislature, epitomizes the dilemma. Gay couples, the court declared, "seek nothing more, nor less, than legal protection and security for their avowed commitment to an intimate and lasting human relationship"; acknowledging that aspiration, it proclaimed, was "simply, when all is said and done, a recognition of our common humanity." The Vermont legislature, for its part, rose to the defense of "a class of people whose civil rights are being trampled upon." Yet *still* the legislature stopped short, contenting itself with granting homosexual couples the same legal rights and protections enjoyed by heterosexual married couples while denying them the right to call it "marriage."

From its own perspective, then, *The New Republic* was surely right when it editorialized that "to grant homosexuals all the substance of marriage while denying them the institution is, in some ways, a purer form of bigotry than denying them any rights at all." For if what is at stake here is, as many liberals argue, a matter of fundamental civil and human rights; if homosexuals deserve to receive the same rights and protections as heterosexuals; if treating homosexuals differently from heterosexuals is inherently discriminatory, bigoted, and irrational; if the love and sexual activity between two men or two women are morally unobjectionable and equal to the love and sexual union of a man and a woman; if it should "no longer be permissible" (in the words of former Vice President Al Gore) "to discriminate against someone because of who he or she falls in love with"; and if we have an obligation to be "inclusive" and thus affirm our "common humanity," then on what moral or intellectual ground can a good liberal oppose same-sex marriages? As best as I can tell, such opposition is based mostly on a feeling, like the feeling of Vermont's Governor Dean, who said defensively that same-sex marriage "makes me uncomfortable, the same as anybody else."

Are there principled grounds for being against gay marriage? Of course there are, and I get to them in the course of this chapter. But before doing so I cannot help pointing out that the decision of the

Vermont supreme court was itself a breathtaking example of judicial overreach. The court contemptuously bypassed the proper avenue by which any such decision should be made—namely, by the people of the state—and forced upon the legislature a straitjacket of only two possible outcomes. And it did not even do so on proper legal grounds, by declaring that the marriage statute being challenged by gay activists violated the Vermont constitution. The court's decision, in short, had no basis in constitutional law; it was, rather, an act of raw political coercion.

There is more to say about the court's opinion. In the matter of child-rearing, it declared heterosexual and homosexual relationships equal, averring that "the laudable governmental goal of promoting a commitment between married couples to promote the security of their children and the community as a whole provides no reasonable basis for denying the legal benefits and protections of marriage to same-sex couples, who are *no differently situated with respect to this goal than their opposite-sex counterparts*" (emphasis added). In so doing, however, the Vermont decision eviscerated any standard the court itself might one day want to invoke when people come forward who similarly profess a deep commitment but who are in sexual arrangements—and one must assume there are some such arrangements—that the court *would* consider objectionable or deviant. Such persons (involved, for argument's sake, in an incestuous relationship) could legitimately declare, after all, that they, too, are "no differently situated with respect to" child-rearing than anyone else. On what basis, therefore, should they be denied the benefits granted to married couples?

While the state legislature passed the civil union bill, and the governor signed it into law, there is no question that the Vermont supreme court was the driving force behind it. In the words of the legal scholar Andrew Koppelman of Northwestern University, the court understood its "power to reshape culture." That it surely did.

Indeed, the history of modern America is, in part, the history of the judiciary's effecting massive social change while the executive and legislative branches sit by or, worse, abdicate their proper responsibility. This has happened in the areas of racial politics and abortion, and it is now happening in the area of homosexuality as well.

Thanks to that fact, Vermont-type civil unions are likely to spread. To understand why, consider an example used by the writer David Frum. Assume that a homosexual who lives in Vermont is hit by a car in, say, Massachusetts, and his partner demands to be recognized as his next of kin. More likely than not, the Massachusetts courts will acknowledge this relationship—at which point, without the legislature or the executive branch or the public itself having lifted a finger, civil unions would now be recognized in Massachusetts. The same sort of scenario might play itself out in many different states. "In other words," Frum writes, "the long-anticipated legal crisis of the American family has arrived."

III

To lay out the case against homosexual marriage, we need to take up the arguments in its favor. Among those arguments, one of the strongest is that far from being a radical act that would subvert traditional cultural norms, same-sex marriage would promote fidelity, responsibility, and stability within the homosexual community itself, thus bringing it into greater conformity with prevailing social standards. Indeed, we are told that same-sex marriage would be a profoundly traditionalizing act—"conservative in the best sense of the word," according to Bruce Bawer, one of its advocates.

The writer Jonathan Rauch likewise believes that gay marriage is compatible with, and indeed would enhance, the pro-family position in American life. He imagines what an enlightened society would say: "We welcome open homosexuals who play by the rules of monogamy, fidelity, and responsibility. And we frown upon heterosexuals and homosexuals who do not play by those rules. We believe that marriage and fidelity are crucial social institutions that channel lust into love and caprice into commitment. We believe faithful relationships are not only good for children but help keep men settled. . . . We support extending these norms to all Americans, gay and straight."

To these proponents, in short, no bad consequences will follow from the legal recognition of homosexual and lesbian marriages. To the contrary, for homosexuals and heterosexuals alike, the consequences can only be good. And that being so, why deny to gays the right to participate in our most cherished and civilizing institution?

As I shall try to show, the "no bad consequences" assertion is deeply wrong. But I also take issue with the implicit notion that what we are talking about is simply adding a new group to the category of married people while keeping intact the essential structure of marriage and family. To the contrary: What is being demanded is the most revolutionary change ever made to our most important institution. One may applaud such a change or one may decry it, but the idea that it is a minor matter, let alone a "conservative" or "traditionalizing" move, is Orwellian.

Consider: If same-sex marriage were to prevail, society would have to accept certain basic assumptions. It would have to accept that the Jewish and Christian understanding of marriage and family life is thoroughly misguided—simply wrong. It would have to accept that humankind itself has been misguided—wrong—to recognize something different, special, or sacred about the sexual union of husband (male) and wife (female). It would have to accept that marriage has nothing to do with the different, complementary nature of men and women. It would have to accept that homosexuality is equal in all important ways to heterosexuality. In short, it would have to accept that marriage is an arbitrary social construct that can be and should be pried apart from its cultural, biological, and religious underpinnings and redefined by anyone laying claim to it.

Nonsense, respond gay rights advocates, especially to the last point. All we are doing, they say, is re-drawing the line so that marriage may now include two (unrelated) members of the same sex, but nothing more. The idea that recognizing same-sex marriages could lead to all sorts of *other* arrangements is reactionary, laughable.

But is it? Say what they will, there are no principled grounds on which advocates of same-sex marriage can oppose the marriage of two consenting brothers. Nor can they (persuasively) explain why we ought to deny a marriage license to three men who want to marry. Or to a man who wants a consensual polygamous arrangement. Or to a father and his adult daughter. Any of these people may desire to enter into a lifetime of loving, faithful commitment; may believe that without marriage their ability to love and to be loved is incomplete, that society is preventing their happiness, and that they deserve to be treated equally by the government to which they pay taxes and bear allegiance. These are the same arguments used by proponents of same-sex marriage to justify their cause. What makes them suddenly illegitimate when invoked by people who engage in polygamy or incest?

Two things, according to Andrew Sullivan, who has written eloquently on this subject. One is that homosexuality is "morally and psychologically" superior to polygamy. Another is that "there is no polygamists' rights organization poised to exploit same-sex marriage to return the republic to polygamous abandon." Jonathan Rauch, for his part, says that homosexuals are asking for the right to marry "not anybody they love, but *somebody* they love." The purpose of secular marriage, he reminds us, is to "bond as many people as possible into committed, stable relationships," and polygamy radically undermines that purpose. "I don't ask to break the rules that we all depend on," Rauch writes. "I just want to be allowed to follow them."

But (to take these arguments in reverse order) Rauch *does* want to break a basic rule we have all depended on, and one that has been in place for millennia, namely, that marriage is by definition the union of a man and a woman, and that its purpose is not the vague wish to "bond as many people as possible" but the quite specific end of procreation and the nurturance of the next generation. This is assuredly not the rule that Rauch "just want[s] to be allowed to follow." And once that rule has been broken, why stop there?

As for the alleged nonexistence of polygamists' rights organizations, to which Andrew Sullivan points, less than three decades ago the same thing could have been said about organizations pressing for homosexual marriage. As we saw in an earlier chapter, polygamy has been far more widely accepted throughout history than homosexuality—and, as it just so happens, polygamists' rights organizations have already been forming today to press for exactly what Sullivan seems to find so unimaginable. According to a recent *Washington Post* story, an estimated thirty thousand people in the western United States live polygamously, and there have been "substantial cracks" in the wall built against polygamy. The Utah chapter of the American Civil Liberties Union argues that the polygamy ban violates citizens' right to privacy and legislates the actions of consenting adults. According to *The Post,* "they liken the ban to sodomy laws, which have been found unconstitutional in states such as Georgia and Texas."

Finally, is it so patently obvious that homosexuality is "morally and psychologically" superior to consensual polygamy? After all, polygamy, too, is undertaken in the name of "bonding as many people as possible into committed, stable relationships," and it has no doubt succeeded from time to time in doing just that. In invoking the "stability" argument, Rauch and Sullivan are thus building a case for a practice they judge "morally and psychologically" inferior to the practice whose cause they propound. They are also inadvertently reminding us why it is that (as Charles Krauthammer has pointed out, and as study after study confirms) most Americans believe *het-ero*sexuality to be "morally and psychologically" superior to homo-sexuality, and why they deny the validity of homosexual marriage.

Having just rewritten the central rule of the marriage bond, proponents of same-sex marriage are hardly qualified to dictate to others what constitutes its central meaning, or why it can be felt only between two human beings, and not more than two. What arguments would they invoke? Tradition? Religion? The time-honored definition of the family? These are the very pillars they have already destroyed. No, once marriage has been detached from the natural, complementary teleology of the sexes, it becomes nothing more than what each of us makes of it. This way, chaos follows: social chaos no less than intellectual and moral chaos.

IV

Which brings us to the claim that, in practice, no bad consequences to the institution of the family would flow from the legalization of same-sex marriage.

Advocates would have us believe that homosexuals do not want any change in the obligations that marriage entails, namely, fidelity and monogamy. This is undoubtedly true for some. But a significant number of others are—as one of their own spokesmen has put it— "no fans" of marriage as currently constructed. Their aim is not the pious (if, as we have seen, disingenuous) one cited by Sullivan and Rauch, namely, being allowed to follow the existing rules. Rather, it is, to quote Michaelangelo Signorile, to "fight for same-sex marriage and its benefits and then, once granted, redefine the institution of marriage completely, to demand the right to marry not as a way of adhering to society's moral codes but rather to debunk a myth and radically alter an archaic institution that as it now stands keeps us down."

Indeed, even some who claim to be more "traditional" in their views find the strictures of family to be too much. Andrew Sullivan, in a candid admission at the end of his book *Virtually Normal: An Argument About Homosexuality*, writes that homosexual marriage contracts will have to entail a greater understanding of the need for "extramarital outlets." Although he has since complained that his words have been taken out of context, those words are in fact consistent with his no less candid—even proud—declaration that homosexuals are "not entirely normal," and that their "essential" and "exhilarating" otherness has to do precisely with their breaking out of the "single, moralistic, model" of heterosexual normality.

But learning to live within the constraints of that "single, moralistic model" is exactly the point of the marriage commitment between a man and a woman, a commitment that does not—that cannot—countenance "extramarital outlets." Marriage by definition is not an "open" contract; its essential idea is fidelity. Obviously that essential idea is not always honored in practice. But it is that to which we commit ourselves. In insisting that marriage accommodate the less restrained sexual practices of homosexual men, Sullivan repudiates the very thing that supposedly has drawn him and others like him to marriage in the first place.*

* Some gay activists understand this very well, and that is why they *reject* same-sex marriage altogether. For them, a vow of monogamy is not worth the price of admission, and they are not willing to pretend otherwise. Thus, Professor Nancy D. Polikoff of American University has lamented the "desire to marry in the lesbian and gay community," which she characterizes as "an attempt to mimic the worst of mainstream society, an effort to fit into an inherently problematic institution that betrays the promise of both lesbian and gay liberation and radical feminism."

Advocates of same-sex marriage concede that at least among male homosexuals, promiscuity *is* a problem—but, they say, it is a problem only because access has been denied to the institution of marriage and would recede once access were granted. This proposition is, at best, an untested hypothesis; we can look to no society to see what the effects of homosexual marriage might be. But that promiscuous sex is among the cornerstones of gay culture is a well-established fact. For many male homosexuals, sexual "liberation" defines their very identity: It is, in a deep sense, what it means to be a homosexual. Nor is it any secret that among the most prominent features of gay urban life is a culture of, in the words of a *New York Times* article, "sex clubs, bathhouses, and weekend-long drug parties where men may have intercourse with a dozen partners a night."

Not all homosexuals participate in this culture, of course; but there can be no denying that it is widely accepted within the homosexual community, and for that matter widely "understood" and condoned by the media. And that is not, I believe, because gay men have been denied access to marriage. AIDS has taken a gruesome toll among male homosexuals, and still promiscuity remains a prominent fact of life among them. As the critic Mark Steyn has written, if "a grisly plague has not furthered the cause of homosexual monogamy," why would "a permit from the town clerk?"

There is also this: Men are in general much more inclined than women to want sex without commitment or restraint—which suggests, as the syndicated columnist Mona Charen has aptly put it, that it is not marriage that domesticates men; it is women. And, I would crucially add, children. For most men, the presence of a child deepens the sense of obligation and responsibility, commitment and fidelity. Yet both women and (for the most part) children would be missing in male homosexual marriages, which again calls into question the degree to which marriage would temper their promiscuity. (The fact that lesbian couples are far more likely than are male homosexuals to live in stable, monogamous relationships is still another indication that the absence of marriage alone cannot explain promiscuity among the latter.) And, in connection with children and promiscuity, I have not said a word yet about the increasingly routine depictions of pedophilia—sex between adult males and boys as young as nine—in mainstream gay fiction and journalism, a phenomenon that, as Mary Eberstadt has pointed out, has gone largely unremarked and (such is the temper of our literary culture) largely uncondemned.

My own guess is that in some cases marriage would indeed restrain some who would otherwise not be inclined to practice self-control. But the notion that vast numbers of homosexual men are longing to adhere to stable, monogamous, lifelong relationships is a fiction. To the contrary, given what we know about gay culture, it is reasonable to surmise that instead of marriage radically tempering homosexual promiscuity, same-sex marriage in practice would lead to the further legitimation of "extramarital outlets" for all.

In any event, encouraging an ethic of monogamy and fidelity in gay culture, laudable as that may be, is a job for homosexual activists themselves, and is still no reason for extending legal recognition to homosexual marriage. Most of us do not see marriage as a matter of harm reduction; it is about much larger things. As a matter of public policy, then, reducing promiscuity among male homosexuals is a less urgent task than strengthening and preserving the institution of marriage and family. That latter task would not be furthered, it would be subverted, by the legitimation of gay marriage.

V

In the early 1990s, *Heather Has Two Mommies* and *Daddy's Roommate*, two books to which I referred earlier in this chapter, formed part of the notorious Children of the Rainbow curriculum proposed by New York City's Board of Education. The stated purpose was to make first-grade children who were being raised in gay and lesbian families feel understood by their teachers and peers. In fact, however, the curriculum went much farther than that, recommending that teachers *initiate* the exploration of gay and lesbian issues in all classrooms as part of an effort to teach that heterosexual and homosexual marriages are equivalent.

Many parents, outraged, fought this effort, and for their pains were denounced as intolerant homophobes. They did eventually prevail—in that instance. But that was almost a decade ago. If same-sex marriages are legally recognized, their fight and the fight of millions of parents like them will become much harder, if not impossible, to conduct. Books like *Heather Has Two Mommies* will then no longer be regarded as anomalies but will more likely be staples of the sex education curriculum, and parents who want their children to be taught the privileged status of heterosexual marriage will not only be portrayed as intolerant bigots, they will necessarily be at odds with the new law of matrimony.

Under such a new regime, homosexual couples would also have equal claim with heterosexual couples in adopting children, forcing us (in law at least) to deny what we know to be true: that it is far better for a child to be raised by a mother and a father than by two homosexuals. What this would mean is that, in the words of David Frum, "our society will be endorsing the conscious creation of families intended from the beginning to be fatherless or motherless or both."

To be sure, proponents of same-sex marriage contend that children raised by gay couples do not suffer adverse effects—another extension of the "no bad consequences" argument. According to Charlotte Patterson, a psychology professor at the University of Virginia, the crucial issue is that children should have the support of loving parents, period, and it does not matter whether those parents are a man and a woman, two men, two women, or whatever. But the research on this matter is very sparse, based on small samples and exceedingly brief periods of study. As James Q. Wilson has written: "The existing studies focus on children born into a heterosexual union that ended in divorce or that was transformed when the mother or father 'came out' as a homosexual. Hardly any research has been done on children acquired at the outset by a homosexual couple. We therefore have no way of knowing how they would behave." Wilson wisely goes on:

> It is one thing to be born into an apparently heterosexual family and then many years later to learn that one of your parents is homosexual. It is quite another to be acquired as an infant from an adoption agency or a parent-for-hire and learn from the first years of life that you are, because of your family's position, radically different from almost all other children you will meet. No one can now say how grievous this would be.

Proponents of gay marriage have an answer to this too. If, they say, we would rather not confer upon homosexual couples an equal claim with heterosexual couples in adopting children, then by all means let us give preference to heterosexual couples, so long as homosexual couples are not excluded altogether. But this is much too breezy. Gay rights activists would surely fight any attempt to restrict homosexual adoption and parenting rights, and courts would find it almost impossible to say no to equal adoption rights once homosexual marriage has achieved equal status in law. We are already seeing a rise in homosexual adoption as the relevant agencies become more willing to accept gay men and lesbians as parents.

We are now coming to the very heart of the matter.

VI

Americans in their overwhelming majority are instinctively tolerant of homosexuality. Their attitude is live and let live. I have already cited the figures arrived at by Alan Wolfe in *One Nation, After All* and seconded by such other recent surveys as a January 2000 poll by the Democratic Leadership Council that found sixty-four percent of Americans believing that "homosexuality is a private matter, not a matter for society to either accept or discourage."

But here's the rub. The stated goal of homosexual activists is not merely tolerance; it is to force society to *accept*. It is normalization, validation, public legitimation, and finally public endorsement. That is a radically different matter. Once we were to codify it in law, we would be saying that homosexual life and heterosexual life are equal in all important respects, that there is nothing special about the union of man and woman in holy matrimony, that there is nothing normative about the role of father and mother in the raising of children. And to those children we would be saying: Your own ultimate sexual orientation is a matter of complete indifference to us.

These concessions are hugely momentous—and they are ones that most people, at a deep, intuitive level, reject. If your fifteen-year-old son came to you to discuss human sexuality, would you be utterly indifferent if he announced he wanted to marry another man? I am sure you would not love him any the less; but my guess is that you would grieve. And that grief would not derive from homophobia or bigotry. It would derive from the fact that he was effectively removing himself from the stream of the generations, from the blessings he would never be able to attain, the ties he would never enjoy or be enlarged by. Even in the unlikely event that you were not disturbed at some level by his proposed transgression of time-honored moral truths, you would know that he was about to enter a world filled with much despair, loneliness, and a fair likelihood of premature death.

But, say those who posit the essential equivalence of homosexuality and heterosexuality, sexual orientation is involuntary, immutable, rooted in nature. Science, they assert, has conclusively demonstrated the biological underpinning of sexual preference—so who are we to contend that one form is better than another? In the words of a spokesman for the Human Rights Campaign: "When people learn that homosexuality is not a choice, they will be more willing to treat us as equal members in society."

But the truth is that we still know very little about the genetic influence on sexual orientation. The idea of a "gay gene" is associated with a much-hyped 1993 study by the National Institutes of Health, but that study did not "prove" the existence of a gene that invariably causes homosexuality, nor did it demonstrate that all gay men have it. What it suggested is that genes play *a* role in influencing the sexual orientation of a significant but still unknown percentage of homosexual men, and that homosexuality may therefore not be *solely* a personal choice.

More recent (1999) research casts doubt on even the modest 1993 findings. In a study published in *Science*, researchers attempting to replicate those earlier findings reported that the "data do not support the presence of a gene of large effect influencing sexual orientation." According to the principal author George Rich, the results of different studies "would suggest that if there is a [genetic] linkage [to homosexuality], it's so weak that it's not important." Indeed, the molecular biologist who led the 1993 research group has himself acknowledged the limits of genes in determining sexual orientation. "Clearly," Dean Hammer told *The Boston Globe*, "there is a lot more than just genes going on."

Here is a simple way to illustrate those limits. Identical twins have an identical genetic makeup; on the assumption that genes are the determinative physiological factor, it would follow that if one identical twin is gay, so very probably will be the other. But according to the most recent studies, there is only about a twenty-five percent chance of this being the case. Although that rate is higher than the one between ordinary (nontwin) brothers, it nevertheless clearly suggests that nongenetic factors are very influential.

There *may* be a genetic predisposition toward homosexuality, then, but there does not appear to be anything close to genetic causation. Nature seems to matter—but so, too, does nurture, in the form of environmental influences and social mores. Which leads to yet one more argument against same-sex marriage. Writing in *Commentary*, E. L. Pattullo, formerly the director of Harvard University's Center for the Behavioral Sciences, said there may be reason to believe that "a very substantial number of people are born with the potential to live either straight or gay lives." As youngsters, he went on, such people "have the capacity to 'choose' [their sexual orientation] in the same sense they 'choose' the character that will mark them as adults—that is, through a sustained, lengthy process of considered and unconsidered behaviors."

What goes into that process of choice? A remarkable 1993 article in *The Washington Post*, based on interviews with fifty teenagers and dozens of school counselors and parents from northern Virginia, offered a few clues. According to the article, teenagers were now saying it had become "cool" for students to proclaim they were gay or bisexual—even if they were not. The culture of gay advocacy, in other words, had clearly begun to influence what Patullo calls the range of "considered and unconsidered behaviors"—leading, not surprisingly, to a doubling in the caseload of teenagers caught in what social workers term "sexual identity crisis." Said one psychologist who worked in the schools: "Everything is front page, gay and homosexual. Kids are jumping on it . . . [counselors] are saying, 'What are we going to do with all these kids proclaiming they are bisexual or homosexual when we know they are not?' " Welcome to a society that proclaims there is no difference between homosexuality and heterosexuality.

If we continue down this path—if every important social institution, invoking genetic predisposition, embraces homosexuality as just another "lifestyle"—we cannot be surprised if many more boys grow up to become gay and many more girls grow up to become lesbian. Is that what we want for our children? If not, should we not begin to think hard about what the institutions of our society are saying to them about life, and choice, and sexuality, and family?

Homosexuals bear a burden, and that burden should evoke compassion. But the fact that someone may be "hardwired" with a predisposition to act in a certain way tells us nothing about what our attitude should be to the act itself. There is much evidence that genetics and family upbringing influence alcoholics, but we still encourage sobriety and discourage drunkenness. A chronic alcoholic (or drug addict) may desperately want to stop but find himself unable to do so. Nevertheless, while remaining tolerant—much too tolerant, some say—on the question of liquor itself, we continue to hold alcoholics accountable for their actions, and we do what we can to help them change their ways. We do not endorse a person's desire to get drunk and stay drunk merely because he may have a genetic predisposition toward alcoholism. And we surely do not demand that society confer its blessing on such behavior.

More broadly, a decent, humane, self-governing society will reject the belief that most human beings—homosexual *or* heterosexual—are slaves to their passions, their desires, their genetic predispositions. Our identities are not defined by sex, nor is sex itself an irresistible force. To believe otherwise is to vitiate the concept of individual responsibility and free will. Although our struggles are not all the same, we all do struggle against every sort of human desire, against our biological impulses, against our emotional longings. We do not abjure the struggle because it is difficult or because we seem to be battling against something deep within us—even if that something is as powerful as sexual desire; even if it seems fundamental to who we are.

VII

And what about love?

"I believe everyone has a right to love and be loved, and nobody on this earth has the right to tell anyone that their love for another human being is morally wrong. . . . How can [conservatives] deny the profound love felt by one human being for another?" Thus spoke the singer/actress Barbra Streisand in defense of same-sex marriage.

No one, however, is denying the "profound love" that may be felt by one human being for another. Homosexuals are free to love one another, live together, engage in sexual relations, cherish each other, and share in each other's personal achievements and professional accomplishments. (Homosexual sex is criminalized in some places in this country, but the statutes are in any case almost always unenforced.) What conservatives and for that matter many liberals wish to turn back is something else: a movement to undo the privileged status of marriage and shatter the conventional understanding of family.

There are, moreover, many "loves" in society that we do not sanctify by marriage: the love of parent for child, of grandchild for grandparent, of brother for sister. The same can be said for the love between devoted lifelong friends, the affection of a teacher for a student, the attachment of minister and parishioner. Indeed, *most* loves find expression through something other than marriage, and they are not considered "lesser" loves because they are unsanctioned by wedding vows.

Of course, in speaking of the "love for another human being," Streisand is no doubt being purposely elliptical: What she really means is sexual love. But—for the reasons I elaborated earlier in discussing such cases as incest and polygamy—even if you were to agree that homosexual love is "as good as" heterosexual love, it would not necessarily follow that the sexual love between two homosexuals must find its expression in matrimony.

As for Streisand's claim that "nobody on this earth" has the right to tell anyone that his love for another human being is morally wrong: In fact, we make moral judgments about love *all the time*. Most people agree, for example, that if Steve, married to Linda, falls deeply and passionately in love with Becky, who is married to Robert, then Steve and Becky's love—if it manifests itself in an extramarital affair—constitutes a painful act of betrayal. If a congressman claims he has fallen in love with an underage male page and engaged in sexual relations with him, then (I hope) someone on earth would object. And if a young actress were to fall in love with Barbra Streisand's husband, James Brolin, and decide to carry on an adulterous relationship with him, Ms. Streisand, too, would probably object—perhaps even on moral grounds.

Love alone, love without context, is far from a reliable guide.

VIII

It is hardly a secret that the disapproval of homosexuality expressed by the majority of Americans can be traced in significant measure to the teachings of the Judeo-Christian tradition. Nor is it a secret that many others, including many gay rights activists, regard those teachings—and contemporary Christians and Jews who adhere to them—as narrow, repressive, and bigoted. That is a calumny; I want to show why.

But first let me dispose of an interesting complication. Some homosexual rights activists and their academic defenders have argued that homosexual practices are *not* inconsistent with biblical doctrine, and that it is a misreading of the text to think that either the Hebrew Bible or the New Testament condemns them. According to this revisionist school—led by, among others, the late historian John Boswell—we must therefore amend our understanding of traditional Jewish and Christian attitudes toward homosexuality.

A full explication of the matter is obviously beyond the scope of this book or my expertise, but let me make several general comments. On the subject of homosexuality, the usual passages cited are, from the Hebrew Bible, Genesis 19:1–29 (the story of Sodom and Gomorrah) and Leviticus 18:22 and 20:13 (the "holiness code"); and, from the New Testament, I Corinthians 6:9–10, I Timothy 1:9–10, and Romans 1:26–27 (the epistles of St. Paul). The first thing to be noted about this handful of texts is that every single one of them condemns homosexual conduct in unqualified terms; there is no Scriptural text, anywhere, that approves of it. And the second thing to be noted is that the Bible says nothing about homosexual *orientation*; its strictures apply only to behavior.

Now let's look more closely at what is generally regarded as the most important biblical text on homosexuality, in the first chapter of Romans. Here is the relevant passage (1:18–32):

The wrath of God is being revealed from heaven against all the godlessness and wickedness of men who suppress the truth by their wickedness, since what may be known about God is plain to them, because God has made it plain to them. . . . For although they knew God, they neither glorified Him as God nor gave thanks to Him, but their thinking became futile and their foolish hearts were darkened. . . . They exchanged the truth of God for a lie, and worshiped and served created things rather than the Creator—Who is forever praised, Amen. Because of this, God gave them over to shameful lusts. Even their women exchanged natural relations for unnatural ones. In the same way the men also abandoned natural relations with women and were inflamed with lust for one another. Men committed indecent acts with other men, and received in themselves the due penalty for their perversion. Furthermore, since they did not think it worthwhile to retain the knowledge of God, He gave them over to a depraved mind, to do what ought not to be done. They have become filled with every kind of wickedness, evil, greed and depravity. They are full of envy, murder, strife, deceit and malice. They are gossips, slanderers, God-haters, insolent, arrogant and boastful; they invent ways of doing evil; they disobey their parents; they are senseless, faithless, heartless, ruthless. . . .

In this passage St. Paul is offering a theological argument. He establishes that God has revealed Himself clearly to humanity, and that therefore those who engage in wicked acts are without excuse, having exchanged "the truth of God for a lie" and turned to idolatry. As a consequence of this rebellion against the Creator, God "gives them up" and allows them to go their own way.

In Paul's theology, then, depravity is the result of a willful alienation from God. Paul then vividly illustrates what he means by human depravity, of which homosexuality is but one example and not the worst one. According to Richard Hays, professor of New Testament at Duke Divinity School, "Paul singles out homosexual intercourse for special attention because he regards it as providing a particularly graphic image of the way in which human fallenness distorts God's created order. . . . When human beings 'exchange' these created roles for homosexual intercourse, they embody the spiritual condition of [all] those who have 'exchanged the truth about God for a lie,' " or have fallen under the power of sin.

Most revisionist scholars do not dispute that these verses condemn homosexual practices but insist that they have to be understood in the context of Paul's overall reasoning, which they interpret differently from Professor Hays. St. Paul's reasoning, they say, is that homosexual conduct is wrong only when you engage in it unnaturally—that is, only if you are by nature a *hetero*sexual. Only then is it a "rebellion" against God. Others, like Peter J. Gomes, a Baptist minister who is professor of Christian morals at Harvard, claim that Paul is merely condemning "lust and sensuality in anyone, including heterosexuals," not homosexuality per se; according to Professor Gomes, it is the "storm troopers of the religious right" who willfully misread the Bible in such a way as to deny that it invites homosexuals "to accept their freedom and responsibility in Christ."

Traditional biblical scholars have answered these arguments definitively. First of all, the whole concept of "sexual orientation" was unknown at the time of Paul. Second, the idea that Paul would give his blessing to homosexual acts for *any* reason is fantastic, and unsupported in any of his other writings. Third, this passage obviously deals not with individual actions but with corporate rebellion against God; in the words of Professor Thomas E. Schmidt: "Paul's concern is not with individuals who deny their true selves but with humanity that first generally and now specifically (and sexually) has replaced a truth with a falsehood."

But the simplest rejoinder is that the revisionist position is at odds with what the entire Bible clearly teaches, namely, that sexual intercourse should take place in the context of the marital union of male and female. To argue otherwise is to argue against the entire weight of Scripture on matters of sexual ethics. I understand that some people do not agree with what the Bible has to say on this matter, or that they may reject biblical authority (and church teaching) altogether. Nor, obviously, do I think that what biblical law forbids—a great many things, after all—is what we should necessarily proscribe in our own laws or customs. But there can be no real debate over the plain meaning of the text.

The Catholic Church, to which I have belonged all my life, has its own teaching in this regard. According to the Church, homosexual acts are contrary to natural law (nature in this usage being identified with the created order) and "under no circumstances can . . . be approved." But the Church recognizes that many men and women who have deep-seated homosexual tendencies "do not choose their homosexual condition; for most of them it is a trial." And the Church teaches the right attitude to bring to this matter: Homosexuals, according to the Catechism, "must be accepted with respect, compassion, and sensitivity."

Again, one may repudiate all this as benighted prejudice, but the teaching itself is crystal-clear. And I would stoutly maintain that it is also very far from being a mere prejudice. Christian teaching on homosexuality derives from the biblical belief that human beings ought to live in accord with God's design. It is based on a deep understanding of the beauty and sacredness of the sexual act, and on a no less deep understanding of the complementarity of the sexes, the conditions under which human beings are meant to live, and the conditions under which human flourishing takes place. Encouraging people to conduct themselves in accordance with these insights can be a profoundly humane and loving act.

By contrast, to argue that "loving others" requires Christians to eschew basic doctrine, withhold judgment, and simply accept people as they are regardless of how they live is a thoroughly modern and thoroughly corrupt view. It is also completely detached from the lives and teachings of Jesus and his apostles. Homosexual activists like to depict these figures as never divisive, always "inclusive"; but it was Jesus, after all, who said, "Do not suppose that I have come to bring peace to the earth. I did not come to bring peace, but a sword," and who in the seventh chapter of Matthew declared, "Many will say to me on that day, 'Lord, Lord, did we not prophesy in your name, and in your name drive out demons and perform many miracles?' Then I will tell them plainly, 'I never knew you. Away from me, you evildoers!' "

I am hardly suggesting that we fallen humans start recklessly hurling epithets at our fellow creatures. For Christians, what is needed in this area, as in all areas, is carefully to balance truth with love, fidelity to Scripture and Church teaching with authentic compassion for others.

IX

The effort to dismiss or, failing that, to rewrite biblical teachings on sexuality in general and homosexuality in particular hardly takes place in a vacuum. It is, rather, part of the broader effort to erase or, failing that, to revise the accumulated wisdom of the ages. But what proponents of same-sex marriage do not seem to appreciate—or willfully ignore—is that for centuries the social normalization of homosexuality has been resisted because for good and sufficient reasons people have considered it to be a threat to the common good, morally objectionable, and a violation of ancient and honored injunctions. Great care and much thought have gone into defining what marriage is and why it is incumbent on us to appreciate its importance and its frailty.

I fully recognize that simply because something was done in the past does not necessarily make it right or prudent or relevant to our times (although I am also unimpressed by those who are quick to ridicule the way previous generations lived). It is true that we have inherited much from the past that is wrong or irrational. But we are also heirs of legacies that are not grounded in irrational prejudice but embody important human realities and hard-won lessons about life and civilization.

In the considered judgment of almost every *modern* society, heterosexual marriage is something special and worth preserving, and homosexual marriage ought to be resisted. James Q. Wilson puts it this way:

> Marriage is a union, sacred to most, that unites a man and woman together for life. It is a sacrament of the Catholic Church and central to every other faith. Is it out of misinformation that every modern society has embraced this view and rejected the alternative? Societies differ greatly in their attitude toward the income people may have, the relations among their various races, and the distribution of political power. But they differ scarcely at all over the distinctions between heterosexual and homosexual couples. The former are overwhelmingly preferred over the latter.

Perhaps these societies know something that many homosexual activists do not. Perhaps their opposition to homosexual marriage has been based not on malicious bigotry but on prudence, on respect for reasoned tradition, and on concern for our common life. Homosexual rights advocates want to undo all that has been settled. *We* know better, they say. Give us license to alter a central human institution that we find inconvenient to our purposes, and you will find the institution itself strengthened as a result.

I dissent. You cannot shatter the conventional definition of marriage, change the rules that govern behavior, endorse practices anti-thetical to the tenets of all the world's major religions, obscure the enormously consequential function of procreation and child-rear-ing—and then cheerfully assert on the basis of no evidence whatso-ever that this will *strengthen* marriage. If we are to decide that marriage needs to be fundamentally amended, surely we should do so only if and when a compelling case has been made for a superior alternative. For homosexuals themselves, gay liberation has wrought much agony, instability, promiscuity, and early death. There is very little in it that recommends itself to the rest of us. And if we are re-sponsible, we will turn away this invitation to experiment cavalierly with our future.

With all due respect to proponents of same-sex marriage, it is also important to say publicly what most of us still believe pri-vately, namely, that marriage between a man and a woman is in every way to be preferred to the marriage of two men or two women. Because there is a natural complementarity between men and women—sexual, emotional, temperamental, spiritual—mar-riage allows for a wholeness and a completeness that cannot be won in any other way. ("For this reason," says Genesis, "a man will leave his father and mother and be united to his wife, and the two will become one flesh.") And, based as it is on the principle of complementarity, marriage is also about a great deal more than love.

That "great deal" encompasses, above all, procreation. The time-less function of marriage is childbearing and child-rearing, and the best arrangement ever developed to that end is the marital union be-tween one man and one woman, channeling reproductive activities in a way that is orderly, responsible, humane, and civilizing. The fact that homosexual marriages would be intrinsically nonprocreative ought to tell us something significant all by itself. Such unions would not only change the fundamental *form* of marriage but pry the institution apart from its key social function.

Well, rejoin homosexual rights activists, if procreation is central to marriage, then for the sake of consistency we should not allow sterile or older couples to marry, either. As debater's points go, this is exceptionally weak. One can believe that procreation is a primary purpose of marriage without insisting that only people who can and will have children be allowed to marry. Aristotle defined nature as "that which is, always or for the most part." A person may be born without a hand, but it remains natural that humans have two hands; a dog with three legs is still a member of the natural category of four-legged creatures. Just so, heterosexual couples who remain childless do not violate the norm, or change the essence, of marriage. Two men who marry do.

An editorial in *Commonweal,* a liberal Catholic magazine, puts it very well:

> Exceptions do not invalidate a norm or the necessity of norms. How some individuals make use of marriage, either volitionally or as the result of some incapacity, does not determine the purpose of that institution. . . . We are all the offspring of a man and a woman, and marriage is the necessary moral and social response to that natural human condition. Consequently, sexual differentiation, even in the absence of the capacity to procreate, conforms to marriage's larger design in a way same-sex unions cannot.

"For this reason," *Commonweal* concludes, "sexual differentiation is marriage's defining boundary, for it is the precondition of marriage's true end." These are words I cannot improve upon.

X

Before drawing this discussion to a close, I need to deal with an objection that has been raised from a different quarter entirely. It has been said that focusing on the alleged threat of homosexual marriage is itself a dodge, an attempt to avoid talking about the *real* threats to the American family, namely, adultery, illegitimacy, and divorce. Thus, David Boaz, executive vice president of the libertarian Cato Institute, has pointed out that Cobb County, Georgia—a suburb of Atlanta—passed a resolution in 1993 declaring homosexual lifestyles incompatible with community standards, yet in that same year the illegitimacy rate in Cobb County was running at twenty percent and there were two-thirds as many divorces as marriages. "Surely," Boaz has written, "the 1,545 unwed mothers and the 2,739 divorcing couples created more social problems in the county than the 300 gay men and women who showed up at a picnic to protest the . . . assault on their rights."

As it happens, I myself made a similar point in a 1994 speech to the Christian Coalition. "I understand the aversion to homosexuality," I said at the time. "I understand the difference between approval and tolerance. But if you look in terms of the damage to the children of America, you cannot compare what the homosexual movement has done . . . with what divorce has done to this society. In terms of the consequences to children, it is not even close."

David Boaz is also right in charging that many American public figures want to avoid the whole subject of divorce. This is true of conservatives as well as of liberals. Too many have had divorces themselves, or know close friends who have, or are worried that making an issue of divorce will turn away voters. I also think that some may fixate on homosexuality because it is so far from anything they themselves could possibly be tempted by (though there are surely also some for whom the opposite is the case).

We *ought* to talk about divorce more often, and more publicly, than we do; see the next chapter in this book. Nor, in criticizing homosexual advocacy, ought we ever go beyond what is merited by the facts. But it is also the case that in society at large and even in law, divorce is still acknowledged to be a fracturing of the marital ideal. It declares that a couple has fallen short of a norm that we still believe to be right, valuable, and worthy of our support. By contrast, proponents and supporters of same-sex marriage want to redefine the norm itself. In that sense at least, homosexual marriage poses the greater threat.

In any event, this is not an either/or proposition. Although we should assuredly make divorce (and adultery) more of an issue in our national political debate, that does not exempt the homosexual rights movement from criticism or resistance. The family is already reeling from the effects of the sexual revolution, which replaced the traditional marriage ethic with a code that has sought to free both marriage and human sexuality itself from restraint and commitment. We have reaped the consequences in promiscuity, adultery, cohabitation, divorce, and out-of-wedlock births. It strikes me as exceedingly imprudent to conduct a radical, untested, and inherently flawed social experiment on an institution so broadly under assault that nevertheless still stands as the keystone in the arch of civilization.

XI

The 1996 Defense of Marriage Act (DOMA) was an attempt to ensure that no state would be forced to recognize a same-sex marriage conducted in another state. It was greeted in the liberal media with abuse. *Washington Post* columnist Richard Cohen attacked the "mindless" and "know-nothing" conservative supporters of DOMA and called the bill itself a "union of unprincipled politics with bigotry" on the part of those willing to "embrace homophobia." Elizabeth Birch of the Human Rights Campaign branded it a "very mean-spirited political ploy." Rabbi David Saperstein, director of the Religious Action Center of Reform Judaism, called DOMA "immoral and unjust," a bill that was about "targeting scapegoats" and would "only serve to codify bigotry."

The least that can be said about such language is that it is intemperate and intolerant. But one need hardly be a liberal or a homosexual activist to be intolerant. If the temptation on this side is to brand those with whom one disagrees as mean-spirited and hateful bigots, the temptation for those who defend traditionalist views is to treat homosexuals as implacable foes and as people with no redeeming qualities. (For an extreme and, thankfully, rare example, I cite the Reverend Fred Phelps of the Westboro Baptist Church in Topeka, Kansas, author of such repellent sentiments as these: "Fags are reprobates" and "God laughs when homosexuals die.") Succumbing to either temptation is wholly unjustified. It is something that needs to be mightily resisted by all—and not merely because it is indecorous. There is a more profound reason, anchored in our understanding of the intrinsic worth of all human beings.

In that spirit, I want to close with a few words addressed specifically to traditionalists, among whom of course I count myself. There are things we owe each other as fellow citizens, certain standards we ought to abide by in democratic discourse. And there are also things we ought to learn from life itself, and from the rich diversity of human experience that it lays before us. We have relatives, friends, acquaintances, colleagues, who are fine, impressive, thoroughly decent individuals—and who may also be gay or lesbian. To them we owe respect, civility, and decency both in private dealings and in public debate. Too often the clash of vastly different worldviews has overridden good judgment and civil expression.

This does not mean, however, that we should give up the fight for the principles on which our civilizations stands, or yield to those who would subvert our moral creed. We must be a tolerant people *and* a people of deep convictions. Even as we affirm the principles of individual freedom and display generosity of spirit—for in America, within very broad limits, people may live as they wish—we need not back away in the face of aggressive efforts to validate and normalize the homosexual lifestyle.

Deep moral convictions are often thought to be antithetical to the spirit of tolerance; in fact, they are not. A very particular and very misguided conception of tolerance holds sway today: the tolerance, rooted in relativism, that proclaims we cannot know right and wrong, that rejects assertions based on inviolable principle, that believes truth is a mere social construction. But this is not tolerance; this is moral exhaustion and sloth. Nor is it even sincere. For what we find in settings where "tolerance" is the chief byword is often something else entirely: College campuses, where the free marketplace of ideas should flourish most impressively, may be the least tolerant places in modern America, places characterized by speech codes, tactics of intimidation, and coerced political conformity.

Properly understood, tolerance means treating people with respect and without malice; it does not require us to dissolve social norms or to weaken our commitment to ancient and honorable beliefs. If, in the debate over homosexuality, we adhere to or even imperfectly approximate *that* kind of tolerance, we will be on the right and true path.

Divorce

I

The story appeared in the July 17, 2000, *People:* "Meg Ryan's Shocking Split." Inside, readers learned of the stunning separation of Hollywood megastar Meg Ryan and actor Dennis Quaid after nine years of marriage.

By all accounts, Ryan and Quaid were one of Hollywood's "golden couples," happily married and devoted parents of an eight-year-old son, Jack. "I loved him [when I married him], and I love him now," Ryan had said of Quaid only a few months earlier. "He is an amazing actor and father. We are a great team." A little later, Quaid told reporters of his longing to spend the summer with his wife and son in Montana. "For me," he said, "family is most important."

But then came the filming of *Proof of Life*, and Meg Ryan met the New Zealand actor Russell Crowe. In June, the two flew to London to shoot extra scenes, and rumors emerged of open displays of affection. On June 28 came the announcement of a separation, and two weeks later Quaid filed for divorce on grounds of "irreconcilable differences."

Associates say Quaid was deeply shaken by his wife's affair. Said his former wife, actress P. J. Soles: "I've never heard him sound so sad. . . . He's very concerned about the effects on his son." But Meg Ryan's mother, Susan Jordan, told reporters that although her daughter's image as America's sweetheart "may never recover," at least she was "being honest" about her feelings. "I think Russell [Crowe] is exciting and is giving her something that was clearly lacking in her marriage," offered Jordan, adding, "Who knows if it will last?"

Six months later, it was over.

In May 1999, former Republican Speaker of the House Newt Gingrich called his mother-in-law, Virginia Ginther, who lives in Ohio, to wish her a happy birthday, and then asked to speak with Marianne, his wife of eighteen years. According to a *Washington Post* account, the eighty-four-year-old Virginia Ginther soon found her daughter in tears: "He doesn't want me as his wife anymore," she blurted out. Mrs. Ginther later said of Gingrich's call: "I think it's terrible when people get away with things like this. We accepted him like a son. It's just unbelievable."

What Gingrich, fifty-six, did not tell his wife in that phone conversation was that he was involved with another woman, thirty-three-year-old Callista Bisek, a staff member of the House Agriculture Committee. According to testimony by Ms. Bisek, the affair had begun in November 1993, apparently while Marianne was visiting her mother in a hospital in Florida. Bisek and Gingrich are now married, he for the third time.

According to friends, Marianne—whom Newt Gingrich in 1994 called his "best friend and closest adviser"—was devastated by the dissolution of her marriage. "I am still shocked that all this is happening," she said months after receiving the news. Gingrich will not talk publicly about the divorce; he says he simply wants to move on.

The personal lives of public figures have long held a fascination for the American public. But although divorce and infidelity still make good fodder for news stories, they have become so commonplace that they hardly merit a raised eyebrow. To my knowledge, not a single word of censure was directed at Meg Ryan for having left her husband and young son for another man. And to the extent that Newt Gingrich was criticized, and he was, it was not for his infidelity or his divorce per se but for his hypocrisy as a champion of "family values" even while he was conducting an affair with a woman twenty-three years his junior.

Gingrich's hypocrisy was disturbing. But so, too, were his actions. This, however, one is not permitted to say in polite company. Occurrences of this nature are purely "personal," one is told, and should be immune to public criticism. In the words of Robert Scheer, a *Los Angeles Times* columnist, we should not condemn Gingrich "but rather welcome [him] back into the forgiving embrace afforded by our common humanity."

I disagree. A sledgehammer is being taken to the American family, and there is no reason in the world why we should be expected to stand by in silence, to say nothing and, above all, to do nothing. It is time for the rules to be reconsidered.

II

Almost every reader of this book has either been divorced or knows a family member or friend who has been divorced. And yet almost every reader of this book over the age of fifty can also remember a time when divorce was not only rare but was regarded as a catastrophic event. If a man divorced his wife for frivolous reasons, or left her for another woman, he was shunned by the community. Those responsible for breaking up marriages were called home wreckers or worse; homes in which parents had divorced were "broken." For most couples, even in the world of Hollywood, divorce was an unthinkable option. If a husband and wife did decide to divorce, they found the process time-consuming, arduous, and often prohibitively expensive.

How the world has changed.

Nothing has done more to undermine family life today than the "divorce revolution," which began roughly thirty-five years ago and is now a prominent and, in the opinion of some, a permanent feature of the American landscape. It has touched the lives of tens of millions of American adults and shattered the lives of many more millions of American children. Aside from its impact on personal and family relations, the divorce revolution has affected child-rearing patterns, personal incomes, labor-force participation, residence patterns, and social indices like education, crime, welfare, out-of-wedlock births, and suicide. Its radiating effects threaten many intact marriages as well; according to the sociologists Paul R. Amato and Alan Booth, "The growing social acceptance of divorce has introduced an element of instability into *all* marriages; even happily married people can no longer assume the lifelong commitment of their spouses."

Yet, perhaps precisely because it is such a commonplace occurrence, divorce is something about which public officials are silent. Even Vice President Dan Quayle, in his famous 1992 "Murphy Brown" speech, went out of his way to point out that the problem he was referring to was out-of-wedlock births, *not* households affected by divorce. And the public seems well pleased with this state of affairs. Even among many committed Christians, the phenomenon of widespread divorce creates little consternation. How many people do you know who would actively try to intervene if friends announced they were splitting up?

Divorce is the elephant in America's living room, the topic nobody wants to talk about. I understand the reluctance. Yet in spite of it, and because of it, we must. As the novelist Pat Conroy has aptly said: "Each divorce is the death of a small civilization." Understanding why so many Americans are relentlessly, willfully, putting to death so many small civilizations is surely a matter that deserves careful consideration.

III

The American political tradition is firmly rooted in the concepts of freedom and liberty, independence and emancipation. These are majestic political sentiments. Yet deep currents of thought that properly shape one area of life can traverse into other areas where, misunderstood and misapplied, they wreak havoc. So it is with the ethic of individualism, which has so powerfully influenced our political life for the better, and our family lives for the worse.

A little-known pamphlet entitled *An Essay on Marriage; or, The Lawfulness of Divorce in Certain Cases Considered*, published just a few years after the Revolutionary War by an anonymous Philadelphia author, helps to illustrate my point. It advanced the case for liberal divorce laws by appealing to America's liberty-loving ways, hoping to extend the blessings of freedom "still further—to those unhappy individuals, mixed among every class of mankind, who are frequently united together in the worst of bondage to each other, occasioned by circumstances not in their power to foresee, or prevent, at the time of their union." Similarly, a young Thomas Jefferson, long before he penned the Declaration of Independence, wrote that "liberty of divorce" both "preserves liberty of affections" and "prevents and cures domestic quarrels."

So it should not come as a surprise to learn that historically, the United States has had higher divorce rates than any other Western nation. Still, if divorce has always been more prevalent here, until a hundred years ago it was also far from common—no doubt thanks in large part to our strong religious and moral traditions—and was in fact strenuously discouraged in law. According to the historian Roderick Phillips (whose work I rely on in this discussion), the New England colonies allowed divorce on two grounds only—adultery and desertion—while the middle colonies (New York, New Jersey, Pennsylvania, and Delaware) were more restrictive still, and the southern colonies (Virginia, North Carolina, South Carolina, Georgia, and Maryland) made no provisions for divorce at all. In this the colonies were following England, where divorce was banned.

The eighteenth century saw some liberalization in these attitudes (England's ban even found its way onto the list of grievances held by the colonists against the Crown), and once America won its independence, there was a sharp upsurge in legislation permitting divorce, though grounds were still usually restricted to adultery, desertion and abandonment, impotence, or extreme cruelty. The upsurge caused alarm in many quarters.

But it was only at the end of the nineteenth century and the beginning of the twentieth that rates of divorce began to rise spectacularly. Between 1870 and 1920, the number increased *fifteenfold*, and by the mid-1920s one out of every seven marriages was ending in dissolution. Although other western countries also experienced a dramatic rise in divorce rates in the early twentieth century, none matched the American phenomenon for sheer size and scale.

What accounted for this explosion? A profound shift in social attitudes is one explanation that has been adduced by scholars. For a number of reasons having to do with changes in both material and cultural circumstances, people became far less willing to endure, and far more willing to terminate, an unsatisfying marriage. A second explanation cites the concomitant liberalization of divorce laws, though the precise effect of this on divorce rates is unclear. And a third argument rests on the development in those years of an early women's liberation movement which, by providing women with greater economic independence, also gave them more confidence to leave a bad marriage. An early twentieth-century professor, sympathetic to this movement, put it in these terms:

> Marriage is no longer the only vocation open to [a wife] and for which she is qualified. She is not forced into marriage as her only means of support. . . . If marriage is a failure, she does not face the alternative of endurance or starvation. The way is open for independent support. . . . She is no longer compelled to accept support or yield to the tyranny of a husband whose conduct is a menace to her health and happiness.

Some in the early twentieth century considered the rise in divorce a long overdue advancement and the only reasonable way to deal with marriages devoid of love and affection. Others viewed it as a threat to the stability of the American family and a pernicious influence on the nation's moral well-being. Among many, the rising divorce rates caused considerable anxiety, prompting efforts to shore up sandbags against the tide. In 1905, President Theodore Roosevelt encouraged the call for uniform divorce laws among the states, decrying the "diminishing regard for the sanctity of the marriage relation." And more than a hundred pieces of antidivorce legislation were in fact enacted between 1884 and 1906, if to little avail.

The aftermath of World War I turned out to be a key moment in the history we are recounting. In the 1920s the number of divorces spiked and then, during the Great Depression of the 1930s, it just as suddenly dropped. The latter phenomenon is the more interesting: Although one might have expected material deprivation on so massive a scale to strain and eventually break many marriages, it seems instead to have caused families to rally together.* (Of course, grinding poverty also made divorce a highly impractical option.) But with the end of the Depression the rates rose again, and by the time of World War II and its immediate aftermath, they had skyrocketed to record levels.

The real break came in the years immediately prior to 1950 and throughout the following decade, years that offered a welcome respite in a century of divorce. This was, indeed, a period characterized by relatively strong, stable families and by a public ethic of marital commitment. In this as in other respects, I might interject, the much-maligned '50s continue to have a great deal to teach us.

As everyone knows, however, the 1950s ethic of marital commitment went out the window by the mid-1960s, and by the 1970s we had embarked upon an authentic revolution in our national manners and mores. More so even than today, divorce in the early 1970s was heralded as a sophisticated and even a morally correct thing to do. Divorce, it was argued, would *strengthen* society. Children would experience "personal growth," while adults who had the "courage" to divorce would not only find personal liberation but become healthier, more fit, more alive. The spirit of the age was encapsulated in the best-selling 1974 book *The Courage to Divorce*, whose authors, two clinical social workers, declared the common effects of divorce to be "essentially nontraumatic":

---

*For a discussion of the converse situation—that is, the special pressures on family life exerted by affluence—see my discussion in Chapter One.

It has been our experience with patients and friends that both spouses, after an initial period of confusion or depression, almost without exception look and feel better than ever before. They act warmer and more related to others emotionally, tap sources of strength they never knew they had, enjoy their careers and their children more, and begin to explore new vocations and hobbies.

With the help of social revolutionaries like these, there came about one of the sharpest, most sustained rises in divorce ever seen in human history. American family life has never been the same.

IV

What exactly do we know about divorce today? As will become apparent later on, we know a great deal about the consequences. But our grasp of the causes of divorce, and of the situations and characteristics of divorcing couples, is not as thickly detailed as it might be. Nevertheless, we do know some things.

We know, for example, that while divorce has dropped since its peak rate in 1980, the United States still has the highest divorce rate among Western nations. We know that in 1998 there were 2.24 million marriages and 1.14 million divorces. We know that if present rates continue, about forty out of every one hundred first marriages will end in divorce, two and a half times the rate only four decades ago.

We also know that more than three-quarters of divorced men and two-thirds of divorced women remarry, and that this remarriage occurs on average within three years. And we know that among women under forty, upward of sixty percent of these remarriages will themselves end in divorce. We know that, for couples who divorce, the median duration of first marriages is approximately eight years; of remarriages, between five and six years; and of third marriages, about three years.

A few other things we know: While the divorce rate increased in all social classes during the 1960s and 1970s, it is higher among people with less education and lower income. But this needs to be qualified. In general, and whatever the income level, two full-time working spouses are much more likely to divorce. Moreover, women who work outside the home are more likely to divorce than those who do not, and highly educated career women (but not men) show a higher rate of divorce than women of lower educational and career levels.

African Americans display higher rates of separation and divorce than do other racial and ethnic groups; Asian Americans show the lowest. People who marry as teenagers divorce much more often than people who marry in their twenties. And, as we saw in Chapter One, couples who cohabit before marriage are almost twice as likely to divorce as those who do not.

More than one million children per year are involved in divorce, a number that has remained relatively stable since the mid-1970s, and more than eight million children are now living with a divorced single parent. About forty percent of children who grew up in the 1980s and early 1990s have witnessed the divorce of their parents—a generation ago the figure was twenty-five percent—and half of all children whose parents remarry will witness a second divorce before they reach the age of eighteen. It is more likely that a child will experience the divorce of his parents than that he will go to college. During the past year, one-third of the children of divorced parents had seen their father only once, if at all, and only one-fourth had seen their father once a week or more. Children of divorced parents tend, themselves, to have weaker commitments to marriage and to be more likely to divorce than children from intact families.

In economic terms, divorce exacts a far greater toll on women than on men. Whereas the average divorced man experiences an *increase* in his standard of living, the average divorced woman, unless she remarries, can expect a precipitous drop in her financial condition and may well end up at or near the poverty level. To make matters worse, of the almost seven million mothers who are separated, divorced, or remarried, fewer than one-third receive the full amount of child support they are owed. Almost forty percent of children living with a divorced mother are in poverty.

These are some of the things we know, and they are dismal.

Given its prevalence, one might expect that research into the causes of divorce would be given the same high priority as, say, research into life-threatening diseases, or the Human Genome Project. But this is hardly the case. We are forced largely to rely on anecdote and random surveys.

What are some of the reasons for divorce cited by divorced couples themselves? A Gallup poll in the late 1980s listed "incompatibility" (forty-seven percent), "infidelity" (seventeen percent), "drug and alcohol abuse" (sixteen percent), "arguments over money, family, and children" (ten percent), and "physical abuse" (five percent). In five percent of the cases, no cause was given. But some scholars question the value of surveys like this, on the grounds that the reasons people give are often constructed after the fact and that the stages of marital dissolution are far less clear than is often supposed. They may well be right.

One of the most puzzling findings is that in those situations where one spouse wants out and the other wants to maintain the marriage, almost seventy percent of the time it is the *woman* who wants out. Since divorce exacts a greater economic toll on women, how do we account for this fact?

One explanation has to do with differing expectations. Some suggest that because women usually have higher hopes from marriage, they may be more easily disappointed. It is certainly true that women tend to be quicker at sensing problems; we often hear of husbands complaining that they had no idea there was anything wrong with their marriage, and of wives at a loss to understand how their husbands could be so blind to what was coming. But Maggie Gallagher, coauthor of *The Case for Marriage*, adduces other factors. Women, she suggests, have been disproportionately affected by the "great American divorce romance"—i.e., the idea that marriage is oppressive to women and that divorce is the way to break free to a new life. In addition, she points out, the rise of women's work has devalued the breadwinning contribution of men, leading some wives to believe that if they divorce, they will not be giving up all that much financially.

An alternative set of explanations focuses on the dynamics of the divorce itself. While, it is said, women may indeed be the initiators, in the final analysis it is men who are often responsible—through the infidelity or emotional abandonment or extreme inattentiveness or actual physical abuse that causes their wives to see the handwriting on the wall. Against this view, still other experts point out that abusive husbands, exploitation, and adultery are actually cited in a relatively small percentage of cases.

A third set of explanations has to do with children and the issue of custody. To Maggie Gallagher, the devaluation of fathering in our culture affects a wife's judgment of the "cost/benefits of marriage" itself, especially if she believes it no longer satisfies her emotional needs. Taking a somewhat different tack, a study by Margaret F. Brinig and Douglas Allen argues that women may initiate a breakup when they are confident they will be able to take their children with them. "The question of custody absolutely swamps all the other variables," according to Dr. Brinig. "Children are the most important asset in a marriage and the partner who expects to get sole custody is by far the most likely to file for divorce." But this can cut either way: Sometimes, though not often, it is the father who is determined to gain custody. (While we are on the subject, it is also appropriate to remind ourselves that whether they have custody or not, many divorced fathers remain zealously committed to their children's welfare.)

All these explanations remain largely speculative. Much more needs to be done before we can say with any real assurance why people divorce in the numbers they do.

V

That divorce is a habit, virtually everyone agrees. The argument begins over whether it is pernicious and damaging. To its defenders, now as in the past, the contrary is true: Divorce, in the words of the liberal writer Katha Pollitt, "is an American value," and one that brings many liberating benefits. As for its putatively negative affects, especially on children, there is, writes Ms. Pollitt, "no study that shows that children do worse in divorce than they do in a really dysfunctional home." Similarly, according to the feminist writer Barbara Ehrenreich, "the alleged psyche-scarring effects of divorce have been grossly exaggerated."

But facts are stubborn things, and if statistics on the *causes* of divorce are not everything they might be, the harmful *effects* of divorce are not "alleged" but empirically demonstrable and thoroughly documented. Although it may well be that "no study" can show that a child would "do worse in divorce" than in a "really" dysfunctional home—say, a home marked by physical abuse and gross parental neglect, in a neighborhood overrun with guns and gangs and drugs—such circumstances are hardly typical. The vast majority of children of divorce do, in fact, suffer, and suffer badly.

Let me begin with the most obvious point: Such children witness the destruction of the most important relationship in their young lives, in almost every case losing the inestimable advantage of having two parents at home to protect, nurture, educate, and guide them. Most also suffer financially, since in the overwhelming number of divorce cases the mother retains custody even though the father has been the main breadwinner.

When parents are in the process of divorcing, children are often party to bitter conflicts and pressured to side with one parent against the other. In the immediate aftermath of a divorce, children often live with a newly single adult who is embittered and depressed, withdrawn and distracted. They face other disruptions as well, often being forced to leave their neighborhood, school, and friends.

As for the longer-term effects of divorce on children, they, too, are many and measurable. Divorce frequently leads to lower educational achievement, higher dropout rates, and problematic work patterns. Children of divorced parents show a greater propensity to commit crimes, use drugs, have out-of-wedlock births, and end up on welfare. They are more likely to become victims of domestic violence and sexual abuse. They have more health problems. They tend to be more depressed, resentful, or withdrawn; to have worse relations with peers and other adults; to show less affection to, and feel less supported by, their parents; and to be more likely to divorce when they themselves marry.

All of this remains true even when you control for race, income, socioeconomic status, and other variables. It is, incidentally, why I believe that we should distinguish between the divorce of a childless couple and one in which children are involved. The former can be harmful to the idea of marital permanence, but the latter should indisputably be our major concern.

But let me enter a number of qualifications as well. First, where children are concerned, divorce is by no means the principal cause of every pathology I have listed, even if it is almost always a significant contributing cause. Second, the long-term harm caused by divorce may not be as great as the short-term harm—though recent studies indicate that a significant minority of children do suffer serious lasting problems. Indeed, Judith Wallerstein, one of the world's foremost authorities on the impact of divorce on children, believes the effects are cumulative and "crescendo" into adulthood. Third, bad outcomes are not preordained: Obviously, there are many examples of children of divorced parents who have grown up to be successful in every imaginable way.

My point is simply this: The odds of growing up emotionally and physically healthier, better educated, and better off financially are much greater if you are not a product of divorce. On the point of emotional health in particular, the searing pain children can suffer in divorce is vividly underscored in a recent book published by the American Counseling Association *Don't Divorce Us!: Kids' Advice to Divorcing Parents.* One young child wrote this:

> When your parents get divorced, I think that most of the time kids get scared and sometimes cry or scream and that can make the parents maybe take out their anger on the kids. Or make your parents yell at each other more. Some kids may think that the dad might hurt the mom. If you could find a way to prevent that, I would buy that book and talk to my divorced parents.

And here is the retrospectively poignant account of a fifty-year-old professional woman:

To this day I can remember how my older brother, younger sister and I learned of the divorce . . . we were called together to talk about Momma and Daddy not loving each other anymore. They were not going to live together anymore. Daddy would be moving out within a few days and we would stay with Momma. Each of my siblings and I felt so violated and so frightened. We cried for most of the evening. That night, we asked each other what we had done to cause the divorce and what we could do to keep Momma and Daddy together.

These are powerful indictments. In response to them, one defender of divorce, Judge Richard A. Posner, conjectures hopefully that "as divorce has become more common," the "stigma" once associated with it has also "declined and with it the harm to children." In other words, the problem has not been divorce per se but, rather, its bad reputation. Posner offers no evidence to support this claim— perhaps because no such evidence exists. In fact, there has never been a time in which *less* stigma was attached to divorce, but no one even remotely acquainted with reality would argue that today's children of divorce are suffering less harm. "In what sense," Judge Posner wonders, "is the divorce rate too high?" Ask those children.

Other defenders of divorce are more subtle. Of course, they concede, it is better for a child to live with parents who have a good marriage. But often the real choice is between living in a two-parent family with lots of conflict and living with a divorced parent in a relatively conflict-free environment. In other words, the threat to children is not divorce but the dissension that can lead to it. This attitude is embodied in the words of the anthropologist Melvin Konner, who has written that "to continue sounding a hysterical alarm about the effects of [divorce on children] without better evidence is simply irresponsible. [Doing so] preserves bad marriages that may harm children more than divorce does, and . . . creates an epidemic of hurtful guilt and shame in many millions of parents who failed at marriage after doing the best they could."

Konner's arguments are both wrong and misleading. He is wrong to say that we need "better evidence." We have reams of data, almost all of them pointing to the deleterious effects of divorce on children. (In this respect, Professor Konner is like a person who, unwilling to face up to the fact that he has a high fever, decides to criticize the thermometer.) And he is misleading in portraying divorce as an act that often benefits a child trapped in his parents' "bad" marriage.

Let me cite but one authoritative source. Paul R. Amato and Alan Booth, authors of *A Generation at Risk,* followed parents and their children over a fifteen-year period, beginning in 1980. Here is what they found: The solid majority of divorces today occur in *low-*conflict marriages. Note that for Amato and Booth a "highly conflicted" marriage can be one in which spouses only so much as disagree with each other "often" or "very often," which may make a low-conflict marriage sound like many people's idea of paradise. The authors conclude quite reasonably that "with marital dissolution becoming increasingly socially acceptable, it is likely that people are leaving marriages at lower thresholds of unhappiness now than in the past"—which, in light of their definitions of low and high conflict, seems another way of saying that more and more people are leaving for trivial and selfish reasons. Although Amato and Booth do not advocate making divorce harder to obtain, their book closes with an admonition: "Spending one-third of one's life living in a marriage that is less than satisfactory in order to benefit children—children that parents elected to bring into the world—is not an unreasonable expectation."

It is worth recalling that Amato once held a very different view, having written in the late 1980s that "no single family type is associated with optimal child development" and that children are "capable of adjusting to a wide range of family forms and circumstances." What changed his mind was evidence: the evidence first of divorce's clear negative impact on children and second of its usually neutral impact on the subsequent happiness of adults.

But what about those adults? As it happens, many women who divorce—as many as eighty percent—report that they are indeed emotionally better off afterward, and so do around fifty percent of men. To defenders of divorce, such statements speak for themselves: The reason divorce is so widespread, they say, is that (a) adults want it and (b) they benefit from it, at least in terms of personal happiness. Or as the novelist Jane Smiley put it recently in *The New York Times,* adopting a realistic tone: "Marrying with the overriding goal of being happy for all of your adult life . . . is a new experiment. Divorce is its corollary."

There is no reason to doubt the word of people who say they are happier after divorcing. Indeed, it makes perfect sense that they would be, having removed themselves from a situation that for one reason or another caused them distress or pain. And yet, interestingly enough, other statistics—health statistics, of both the physical and the psychological variety—tell a different tale.

Those who divorce are far more likely to experience stress-related physical and emotional illness, to engage in substance abuse, and to display risky behaviors that can dramatically shorten their lives. They are also three times more likely to commit suicide than are married people, and have a forty percent greater risk of premature death. (In the words of John J. DiIulio, "Getting a divorce is only slightly less harmful to your health than smoking a pack or more of cigarettes per day.") And, as I have already noted, the ma-

jority of women who divorce suffer significant financial losses, and
many slide into poverty.

There are also societywide costs of divorce, including an increase in crime, drug use, and prison cells; a rise in the numbers of
welfare recipients, out-of-wedlock births, and abused children; a decrease in educational achievement and high school graduation rates;
and larger expenditures on medical care, day care, child support, and
remedial education. The fact that children of divorced parents
themselves end up divorcing more frequently contributes to the per-
petuation of marital instability throughout society—yet another indication of the interconnectedness of the issues we have been
discussing in this book.

Do the facts and figures I have adduced in the preceding pages
mean that divorce is *always* wrong and unwise? Of course not. Some
marriages are irretrievably broken, destroyed by infidelity, fraught
with conflict and anger and maybe even physical abuse. Many of
these kinds of marriage ought to end in divorce. Nor should critics
pretend that people who divorce always do so for frivolous or self-
indulgent reasons, or will live only to regret it. Any number of people who feel trapped, or who believe they made a mistake marrying
someone with whom they are profoundly incompatible, eventually
divorce and later remarry and in so doing find greater personal happiness and fulfillment. Their children, after a period of turmoil, also
seem to adjust relatively well. And so, in fact, does the divorced
spouse. What should a critic say then?

I myself would begin by pointing out that divorce still entails
the breaking of a solemn vow, made to one another and before God,
to remain as man and wife "till death do us part." And I persist in
my belief that in the vast majority of circumstances, breaking this

vow is a morally troubling thing. But even putting aside my retro-
grade convictions, there are other points to be made.

In most marriages on the edge of breakup, one spouse wants to
divorce and the other does not; it seems to me that we ought to be
more solicitous of those trying to save a marriage than of those trying to end it. Then, too, although happy-ending scenarios obviously
do occur, the data I have presented tell us quite unequivocally that
in general, people who divorce and remarry tend to find no greater
happiness than before, and also that the divorce rate for second
marriages is *higher* than for first. This may indicate something
about the utopian expectations of life that, both for good and for ill,
many Americans persist in entertaining; but that is a subject for
another day.

Finally, and most important, a situation that seems very bleak often changes for the better. Eighty-six percent of unhappily married
people who stay together find that five years later their marriages are
happier. And three-quarters of people who have characterized their
marriages as "very unhappy" but have nevertheless remained together report five years later that the same marriages are either
"very happy" or "quite happy"—meaning that (in the words of
Maggie Gallagher and Linda J. Waite) "permanent marital unhappiness is surprisingly rare among the couples who stick it out."

We can sketch any number of scenarios to make divorce appear a
reasonable and even desirable choice. But we need to come to grips
with the fact that somewhere along the way, something has gone
terribly wrong. Sacred commitments have been attenuated. Adults
have elevated their own desires above the pressing needs of children.
And love now has many fewer safe, permanent harbors in which to
reside. We are at a point where millions of us willfully and promiscuously sever the deepest bonds of human affection, and in doing so
inflict a vast amount of human suffering.

How do we extricate ourselves?

VI

David Witham was devastated when his wife, Beth, told him she had met another man and was moving out. According to a *Washington Post* story, Witham "tried desperately to persuade her to stay," but after a few weeks she filed for divorce and in less than a month their eleven-year marriage was over. Witham, stunned, argues that if he had had more time, he might have been able to change her mind. "If divorce was harder to get," he is quoted as saying, "people may find out they can actually work it out. I would have liked to see anything delay the process."

In response to America's divorce epidemic, attention has recently been focused on the possibility of various legislative reforms to make divorce, in David Witham's words, "harder to get." Most of them revolve around changes to the particular divorce system that has been in place in this country roughly since 1970. For it was then that California Governor Ronald Reagan signed into law the nation's first "no fault" divorce law. By 1977, forty-seven of the fifty states had repealed fault grounds for divorce. In less than a decade, the entire legal divorce regime, in almost every state in the union, had been fundamentally changed.

Precisely what was it that thirty years ago people were rebelling *against*? The conceptual basis of our old, "fault-oriented" laws was that marriage ought to be, in almost all instances, an indissoluble union, and divorce exceedingly rare and attainable only on serious grounds (e.g., adultery, desertion, mental cruelty). The system was tethered to the principle of moral and legal accountability—in this instance, holding responsible a spouse who committed a serious marital offense. It also rested on the assumption that when divorce did occur, it ought to be based on mutual consent, thus giving bargaining power to the partner who did not want the marriage to end.

But, since fault had to be demonstrated in every instance, critics contended that our traditional divorce laws created undue antagonism between the divorcing couple. Moreover, because not every divorce involved misconduct, many people were being compelled to resort to perjury and collusion. According to the early advocates of no-fault divorce, "marriages broke up in a context of conflicts in attitude, personality, or other difficulty on both sides, rather than as a result of fault by one spouse and innocence by the other." This meant that the traditional legal approach, "based only upon a matrimonial offense committed by one or both of the parties, [was] essentially outmoded and irrelevant, often producing cruel and unworkable results."

These advocates prevailed in stunning fashion. In state after state, at the stroke of a pen, virtually every legal obstacle to divorce vanished.

At the time, the establishment of no-fault divorce was almost universally regarded as a huge social advance, and one involving few if any costs. We were assured that it would be invoked only in limited circumstances, and that it could not fail to lead to an increase in net marital happiness. The typical attitude was expressed by a woman who said, "I was so relieved when I found out that it didn't matter why I wanted the divorce, that I didn't have to justify it to anyone. . . . It was my choice. That's the way it should be. It's a private, personal decision."

But all such comforting ideas proved illusory. Today, there are as many unhappy marriages as ever, and, to judge by the divorce statistics, far fewer happy ones. In the words of Professor Allen Parkman: "Seldom in U.S. history have laws been enacted with higher hopes and poorer results than the no-fault divorce statutes."

Still, many who concede that little good has come of no-fault divorce laws are against repealing them outright. Such roll-back legislation, they argue, would have virtually no effect on divorce rates and might itself do more harm than good. It would place women with abusive husbands in greater danger by forcing them into conflict-ridden circumstances, fuel lingering anger and resentment between former spouses, divide the loyalties of children, and hurt financially those involved in contested cases by requiring payments to lawyers, therapists, private investigators, pension specialists, and witnesses. Still others argue that one thing we should have learned over the last thirty years is that government has no business interfering in the private (married) lives of men and women.

To take the last point first, the notion that divorce is merely a private, personal decision and therefore ought to be free from government interference is wrong, I think, on several counts. The marriage ceremony itself is a public act and a legal commitment. Moreover, as I have documented, widespread divorce has profound public consequences. Surely society ought to have a say in such matters; indeed, there are few issues in which the state has a *greater* interest than in promoting family stability and permanence.

The government already regulates family life in any number of ways, including by limiting the number of spouses you can marry and specifying a minimum age, by requiring a license (and in some states a blood test) before marriage, and stipulating the terms of divorce (e.g., child custody, child support, and the allocation of property). The question, then, is not *whether* the government should be involved—most Americans believe it should be—but what is the proper scope and nature of its involvement.

I believe we should repeal no-fault divorce, and I am convinced that doing so would lower divorce rates—for the simple reason that it would make divorce harder to attain and less attractive to pursue. Of course, many will divorce no matter how many obstacles are put in their way. But others, who are leaning toward divorce but not finally decided on it, might be deterred. William Galston, who was a top domestic policy adviser in the Clinton White House, has cited a fifty-state study published in the *Journal of Marriage and the*

Family that concluded: "The switch from fault divorce law to no-fault divorce law led to a measurable increase in the divorce rate." It stands to reason that in this case, a properly modified move to turn back the clock may have a similar effect in the opposite direction.

I am not aware of credible evidence showing that no-fault laws have made divorce less acrimonious or caused the anger between spouses to dissipate any faster. Nor should they have; it is not the courtroom proceeding but divorce itself that inflicts acute, lasting damage. Here's a thought experiment: Assume that a wife and mother of three children—ages four, seven, and eleven—is abandoned by her husband after fifteen years of marriage because he decides he wants to start his life anew. Assume also that this wife graduated with honors from the University of Virginia law school and gave up a promising career and hundreds of thousands of dollars in income to stay home with their children. Suddenly she is left alone, and must now give up caring for the children she loves in order to take a full-time job, even though she has been out of the labor market for a decade and a half. Are we to believe that allowing such a husband to divorce such a wife under a no-fault regime would make for *less* anger and bitterness than under a fault system?

According to Judith Wallerstein and Sandra Blakeslee, the authors of *Second Chances: Men, Women and Children a Decade After Divorce,* "One-half of the women and one-third of the men are still intensely angry at their former spouses" after the passage of ten full years. Wallerstein and Blakeslee themselves call this finding "incredible." Whether incredible or not, the effects of the anger they describe are palpable, and not only on the adults. Such anger, write the authors, "has become an ongoing, and sometimes dominant, presence in their children's lives as well."

Now consider the argument that ending no-fault divorce would trap battered women in miserable and abusive relationships. The hidden premise here is that marriage itself is a breeding ground for domestic violence; therefore, the weaker the institution, the better off women will be.

The truth is, however, that husbands are much less likely to engage in domestic violence than are boyfriends and ex-spouses. This kind of violence is a serious problem, but anyone concerned about it ought to become a vocal critic of cohabitation, since women in that situation are at least twice as likely to be victims of domestic violence as are wives. Indeed, reinstituting fault could *help* wives trapped in abusive relationships by providing them with favorable financial consideration during the settlement phase and thus holding out the possibility of greater economic independence.

And this raises another point. Thanks to no-fault divorce, many more women are in the labor force than would otherwise be the case. Such women are in a double bind. Under our no-fault regime a wife has less confidence than ever that her marriage will last, and she cannot hope to gain a favorable settlement should it end. It seems to me that this in itself constitutes sufficient, substantive grounds to favor repeal of no-fault divorce—at least in those instances where children under eighteen are involved.

Still another benefit: Under current law, the spouse who is wronged, or who wants to save the marriage, has *no* negotiating power. Everything favors the party who wants to end matters—and currently eighty percent of all marriages end unilaterally. Under a fault regime, divorce would occur on terms much more favorable to the other partner, which is often the sensible and just way.

And a final consideration: The law is a vital teacher, one that helps shape public attitudes and expectations and that expresses a nation's deep moral convictions. Currently, the law does nothing to discourage divorce, and subverts the idea of marital permanence. It makes it as easy as possible to walk away from the most fundamental of human obligations. You cannot claim a high purpose for marriage and family life while mocking and trivializing them in law, but that is precisely what we are now doing. In America today (to paraphrase Maggie Gallagher), it can be harder to fire an employee of three months' standing than to divorce the mother of your three young children to whom you have been married for ten years.

Repealing no-fault would not necessarily mean returning to the system it replaced. A number of proposals have been floated, including mandatory counseling, "cooling-off" periods, and "covenant marriages." Linda J. Waite and Maggie Gallagher, strong critics of no-fault divorce, have suggested long waiting periods in contested cases, especially for couples with minor children or when one spouse (usually the wife) has been financially dependent on the other for a long time. "Before no-fault," they remind us, such waiting periods "were common in the United States." Their clear advantage is that they slow the rush to divorce, acknowledge that divorce is not simply a "right," and give time to the spouse who is being left to recover emotionally before the legal process begins.

Perhaps, as some have said, the law is among the weakest tools we have to lower divorce rates. But no-fault divorce remains an important bulwark of the divorce culture, and it should be repealed.

VII

Manners are more important than laws, Edmund Burke famously wrote, and this axiom surely applies to marriage and divorce. If we hope to revivify family life, we must look to but also beyond legal reforms. The more important task is publicly to reaffirm the centrality of the family and reestablish cultural strictures against its dissolution.

In America, one institution can do this more effectively than any other: Christian churches, to which more than sixty percent of the American people belong. But there is a hitch. Although one might think that divorce would be much less rampant among practicing Christians than among lapsed or non-Christians, that is far from the case. According to some studies, indeed, "born-again" Christians, who are rightly considered to be among the more pious, are also somewhat more likely to divorce, and this includes persons in positions of religious leadership. Despite its "churchgoing ways," the divorce rate in the Bible belt is higher than in any other region in the country.

In May 2000, *The Atlanta Journal and Constitution* reported the divorce of the Reverend Charles Stanley, a former president of the Southern Baptist Convention, best-selling author, head of a $40-million radio and television ministry, pastor of the 13,000-plus-member First Baptist Church in Atlanta, and a man who had been married to the same woman for forty-four years. The breakup of a marriage, particularly one of more than four decades' duration, is a tragic occurrence. But what makes this incident culturally noteworthy is the *defense* offered by the religious leadership at the conservative First Baptist Church. "In many ways, this experience . . . has prepared Dr. Stanley in a unique way to minister to us and to the world," the Reverend Gearl Spicer told the congregation. "It is my biblical, spiritual, and personal conviction that God has positioned Dr. Stanley in a place where his personal pain has validated his ability to minister to all of us."

One might have expected to hear that a pastor who divorces should resign from the ministry, as many Christian denominations—including most Baptists—believe. (In the past, the Reverend Stanley himself had publicly taught that a divorced man was disqualified from serving as pastor.) At the very least, one might have expected to hear that the Reverend Stanley should take a temporary leave of absence from the ministry, as several evangelical leaders had counseled him to do. One might even conceive of someone arguing that he deserved to remain as minister *despite* the divorce. But one heard none of these things. Instead, the case being made was that divorce would turn Reverend Stanley into a better minister. By this twisted logic, the more broken marriages among ministers, the better equipped they will be to serve.

How is it that divorce has become so prevalent among practicing Christians? The answer varies from denomination to denomination, region to region, and church to church. But we can, I think, offer some generalizations.

Mike and Harriet McManus head a "lay ministry" called Marriage Savers. In recent decades, they say, churches have not done nearly enough on a simple practical level to prepare couples for marriage, to help married couples strengthen and enrich their relationships, or to provide adequate assistance and good counseling to couples experiencing difficulties. (Mike McManus, a Protestant, points out that the Catholic Church has done better on this front than other churches.) In addition, some ministers have shied away from preaching against divorce so as not to appear overly "judgmental" or to offend the many divorced couples in their congregations.

Of greater importance, I would argue, is the degree to which many Christians have absorbed the contemporary ethic of the self and its precepts that I spoke about in Chapter One. We are, in general, less willing than we once were to sacrifice or to keep commitments. We place higher value than ever before on "personal growth," self-expression, and self-discovery. And so we are able, with alarming ease, to abandon a marriage partner whom we view as an obstacle to achieving these things. At the same time, the sexual revolution, and all that followed in its wake, has seriously eroded the Church's moral authority and confidence; in its attempts to accommodate itself to modern culture, Christendom has lost much of its faith in Church doctrine and biblical teaching.

Some Christians have persuaded themselves that a permissive attitude toward divorce is an enlightened accommodation to both human nature and modern life. The retired Episcopal bishop of Newark, John Shelby Spong, is one of them. To him, "alienation," the "inability to communicate," "radically different life paths," and a marriage that has become "less than ultimate" are sufficient grounds not simply to end a union but to *bless* its dissolution. I emphatically disagree. I believe, rather, that something precious is being lost in our easy acceptance of divorce, and that we must redouble our efforts to defend marital permanence as an attainable ideal.

I say this with some understanding of the difficult circumstances many individuals find themselves in. The Church has an obligation not to ostracize or shame people who seek divorce as a desperate last measure and after years of effort but, rather, to stand beside them and offer support and gracious care. But that is not the same thing as being silent on the issue of divorce itself.

Barbara Dafoe Whitehead cites a churchgoing woman who told her the following:

> My husband left our marriage because he met someone he liked better, and she left her marriage because she liked my husband. My husband married this woman, and they broke up two marriages involving five children. And now they go to my church. They sit in a certain pew at church, and I sit there, too, next to my kids. And my church doesn't have anything to say about the right or wrong of their actions.

In Christian teaching, marriage is a sacred covenant before God and divorce a contradiction of His will. To this day, the Catholic Church teaches that divorce is immoral, an act that both violates the natural order and introduces *dis*order into families and into society. Some people may think that such attitudes (like the attitudes of Christianity toward homosexuality) are of almost no relevance to contemporary American society. But for those of us who are convinced that they are expressions of deep, enduring truths about how men and women ought to order their lives, the mandate is clear: We must attempt to shape a society anchored in these truths.

If we hope to reverse the tide of divorce and bind up the social wounds it has caused, America's churches will have to lead. They have led in the past on any number of important issues, including slavery and civil rights. We need them to do so again.

VIII

But the job is not for the churches alone; the job is for all of us. The divorce culture is built on a deeply ingrained philosophy that glorifies personal choice, autonomy, radical individualism, self-expression, and freedom from constraints. If there is thus no great mystery about what will be required if we hope to slow or halt this modern epidemic—mutual sacrifice and fidelity, self-denial and resolve, patience and forgiveness—the task will hardly be easy; for more than three decades we have been relentlessly conditioned to think and to behave otherwise.

Here is precisely the sort of thing I am talking about. Two years ago, Tatiana Namath, the wife of former NFL great Joe Namath, divorced him after fourteen years of marriage. Her reason? "Joe has lived an exciting life, so he's happy to relax now," she said. "I had children at twenty-four, and I've grown in a way that I'd like to be more stimulated." Tatiana Namath, mother of two daughters, aged thirteen and eight, justified her divorce this way: "It's better for my kids to see me happy and fulfilled."

Although Tatiana Namath may not know better, she should. The modern divorce revolution was built on fraudulent claims. It promised that the vast majority of divorces would be liberating, pain-free, and, for women, both emotionally and financially beneficial. We were assured that children would do just as well when raised by one parent as by two. We were told that easy divorce would increase overall marital happiness, and that society itself would thereby gain.

Thirty years later, after the carnage, our excuses have run out. Yes, some people have benefited but fewer, and at a higher cost, than anybody could have imagined.

Evolutionary biologists tell us that both women and men, but especially men, are naturally promiscuous; they also assure us that a sexually exclusive, lifelong commitment is unnatural. Be that as it may, part of what it means to be a morally responsible human is to act in ways that are, sometimes, contrary to our "natural" instincts. If we hope to preserve the humanly ennobling qualities associated with marriage and family life—monogamy, lifetime commitment, child-centeredness—we have to be prepared to repel assaults, including those mounted under the banner of "nature." Otherwise we do not deserve the title of human beings.

In the long run, we need to do even more than answer false arguments and advance correct ones. We need to have in mind a different and better ideal and act in such a way as to proceed in its direction. Our purpose must be to restore marriage and family life to a healthy and vital state, to have families characterized by understanding and affection, intimacy and honesty, forgiveness and the willingness to resolve conflict. And *this* entails creating both a cultural and a social infrastructure to help young people prepare for, and look with anticipation toward, marriage and parenthood. It entails introducing them to the joys and rewards of wedded life, preparing them for its challenges, and equipping them with the wherewithal to make it through the difficult times.

Fortunately, there is emerging a vibrant and far-reaching "marriage movement" in America that is pursuing just these sorts of ends. And we can also take encouragement from the recent shift in the debate about divorce itself. More and more Americans sense, at least in the abstract, that something quite bad is going on. ("New research says the long-term damage [to children] is worse than you thought," confirms *Time* magazine in a September 2000 cover story.) A majority of the public thinks that it should be harder than it now is for married couples with young children to separate. The days when divorce was celebrated as a social advance of the first order are about over.

This shift in attitude helps, but it is not sufficient. Let me offer an analogy from a job I once held in government. The recognition that one has a drug problem is the first step toward recovery. But much more is required. The addict still needs to *act*. Right conduct remains the only true test of resolve.

A Few Home Truths

I

In 1861, at the outbreak of the Civil War, Major Sullivan Ballou, a young Providence lawyer and former speaker of Rhode Island's House of Representatives, interrupted a promising political carrier to join the 2nd Rhode Island Volunteers. From a camp near Washington one week before the first battle of Bull Run, the first major land battle of the war, he wrote home with premonitions of death to his wife, Sarah:

> Sarah, my love for you is deathless. It seems to bind me with mighty cables that nothing but Omnipotence could break; and yet my love of Country comes over me like a strong wind and burns me unresistibly on with all these chains to the battlefield.
>
> The memories of the blissful moments I have spent with you come creeping over me, and I feel most gratified to God and to you that I have enjoyed them so long. And hard

it is for me to give them up and burn to ashes the hopes of future years, when, God willing, we might still have lived and loved together, and seen our sons grown up to honorable manhood around us. I have, I know, but few and small claims upon Divine Providence, but something whispers to me—perhaps it is the wafted prayer of my little Edgar—that I shall return to my loved ones unharmed. If I do not, my dear Sarah, never forget how much I love you, and when my last breath escapes me on the battlefield, it will whisper your name. Forgive my many faults, and the many pains I have caused you. How thoughtless and foolish I have often times been! How gladly would I wash out with my tears every little spot upon your happiness, and struggle with all the misfortunes of this world to shield you and your children from harm. But I cannot. I must watch you from the Spiritland and hover near you, while you buffet the storm, with your precious little freight, and wait with sad patience till we meet to part no more. . . .

As for my little boys—they will grow up as I have done, and never know a father's love and care. Little Willie is too young to remember me long, and my blue-eyed Edgar will keep my frolics with him among the dim memories of childhood. Sarah, I have unlimited confidence in your maternal care and your development of their character, and feel that God will bless you in your holy work.

Tell my two Mothers I call God's blessing upon them. O! Sarah. I wait for you there; come to me and lead thither my children.

A week later, Sullivan Ballou was killed at Bull Run.

———

Six years before his death in 1919, looking back on a lifetime of great goals, lofty and coveted honors, and the performance of many a mighty deed in the public arena, Theodore Roosevelt meditated on earthly achievement:

> There are many kinds of success in life worth having. It is exceedingly interesting and attractive to be a successful business man, or railroad man, or farmer, or a successful lawyer or doctor; or a writer, or a President, or a ranchman, or the colonel of a fighting regiment, or to kill grizzly bears and lions. But for unflagging interest and enjoyment, a household of children, if things go reasonably well, certainly makes all other forms of success and achievement lose their importance by comparison.

These two documents, both from bygone eras in our country's history, and very dissimilar in their tone and approach, address a common theme: what the philosopher Michel de Montaigne called the marks of true and solid contentment. It is a theme that tends to get lost in recitations of facts and figures about marriage and the family, and even in some discussions, like our own, of their indispensable role in the preservation of society and civilization. And yet we must never forget that *this*—true and solid human contentment—is what marriage and family are about.

Major Ballou, placed by destiny at a moment of approaching mortality, reached into his inmost soul for the truths—the home truths—that, having given meaning and purpose to his own life, would also outlast him, comforting and inspiring those he was about to leave behind; and then he found the language, intimate and elevated at once, with which to express those truths. It is the same with Teddy Roosevelt, the bluff man of action with the plainspoken style. Unlike Major Ballou, Roosevelt does not invoke God or Providence or the transporting rewards of eternity but, rather, such mundane categories as career, worldly success, and "enjoyment." But in striking the balance sheet of life, he, too, reaches for some vantage point from which to weigh the value of our strivings, and finds it again in the same home truths.

For most of us at the dawn of the new millennium, it has become very difficult to speak of these truths with anything approaching the simple conviction of a Theodore Roosevelt, let alone the sublime faith of a Sullivan Ballou. It is not just that we have witnessed so much degradation in the very institution—the family—in which they both put their ultimate trust. It is also that we live in an age in which almost *every* human arrangement, from the political to the social to the religious to the moral, has been made subject to corrosive doubt and suspicion and has been presumed guilty until proved innocent—and scarcely a one (to quote Hamlet) has 'scaped whipping. Thus it is that along with the language in which to express it, many of us have quite naturally lost our faith in marriage and the family; and for some of us, reading the words of Major Ballou and Teddy Roosevelt, it may even be hard to remember what it was like to *have* such faith.

Let me try, then, in the driest, most matter-of-fact language I can summon, to rehearse a few home truths about marriage and the family that have come down to us from our long sojourn on earth—and then let me try, however imperfectly, to recapture a few of the ideas and the ideals they rest upon.

II

Marriage and family are cultural universals. Everywhere, throughout history, they have been viewed as the standard to which most humans should aspire. This is not happenstance; it is, rather, a natural response to basic human needs—basic to individuals, and basic to society.

How do marriage and family answer to basic human and social needs? For one thing, as the anthropologists remind us, the marriage of one man and one woman establishes an intricate network of relatives and "kinsmen"—and, with this, certain built-in expectations, reciprocal obligations, and formal responsibilities. Scholars point to the historical dimension of this vital social function. "They are our enemies, and so we marry them" is how the Zulus express the age-old practice of creating, through marriage, powerful alliances among groups that might otherwise have been strangers or even enemies (in French, the word *alliance* still refers to marriage). Similarly, it has been suggested, the reason behind the universal prohibition of incest may have to do not just with avoiding harmful genetic consequences but with encouraging the domestication, as it were, of disparate and potentially warring lineages.

For us, today, the "kinsman" aspect of marriage and family operates in different but still clearly related ways. When you marry, people previously unknown to you take on a special place in your life and have certain claims on you, not because of who they are, but because of the title they bear: cousin, daughter-in-law, uncle. That is what it means to be part of a family, a condition whose liabilities have long been the stuff of folklore and countless in-law jokes, but whose benefits are similarly a matter of indisputable record.

David W. Murray, whose work has heavily influenced my thinking on this subject, says that when men and women marry, they acquire, for better and for worse, all the "entangled wiring" of each other's families. A marriage, in other words, is not merely an exchange of vows between two individual people but an extraordinary social moment in which two different families and sets of friends come together in a "relationship of affinity" based on a formal, publicly recognized, legal commitment. This "entanglement," Murray writes, "is stabilizing—not only in the life of the couple and their children, but in the life of the neighborhood."

That is one practical benefit: When you marry, you gain an economic and social support system. Relations among friends—even very good friends—tend to be more contingent and less dependable than relations among family members. Friends can easily drop out of your life; relatives are usually there for the duration.

Assume, for example, that you were in desperate need of an organ transplant. Your best friend *might* be willing to donate his kidney to save your life, but such a gesture would be an unexpected and quite extraordinary act of generosity. With family members things are altogether different. There is an inherent "should-ness" to family that is found in no other human arrangement.

Or consider a less dramatic but far more common scenario: A friend who is intelligent, energetic, and ambitious but who, in order to advance professionally, needs to borrow $30,000 to complete his graduate degree. To whom will he more readily and naturally turn? To you, his friend, or, like so many of us, to his in-laws? The answer is obvious. And now suppose this same friend is living with a young woman to whom he is not married. Will he *then* turn to her parents for financial help? The answer, to put it mildly, is far less obvious.

Whether we are talking about medical needs or home loans, college tuition, cash help, child care, health care, emergency shelter, access to transportation, or so much else, marriage and family provide a more extensive and reliable support system than is available to the unmarried. Most of us recognize an obligation, unstated but real, to look after the well-being of those to whom we are related, whether we are fond of them or not. Robert Frost once described home as "the place where, when you have to go there, they have to take you in." Family is like that: It creates ties that include, but run much deeper than, personal preference.

Marriage and family perform other functions as well. Families place upon us certain expectations—including, as was once commonly understood, the expectation that we will not bring dishonor upon the family name. To put it positively, the fact that we represent not only ourselves but our families can be a source of authentic pride, and authentic pride (as opposed to false pride) is a powerful motivator of right conduct.

Marriage and family help establish rules for sexual conduct. Throughout all time, societies have known that sex is not only the most powerful of human passions but an activity whose repercussions can be hugely destructive, wrecking human lives and inflicting wounds that can easily last a lifetime. That is why all societies have undertaken to guide sexuality by means of ritual and law.

Marriage establishes a sexual framework that is at once restrictive and liberating. At once, it enables and it sets boundaries. In George Gilder's pithy words, "Under a regime of monogamy there are limits. One may covet one's neighbor's wife . . . but one generally leaves it at that." But under this selfsame "regime," a married couple can be both intimate and open, freed from the intense competition that is an intrinsic element of male-female relations. In marriage, our sexual needs are directed toward emotionally and morally constructive ends.

But the chief argument in the anthropological case for marriage has to do with, precisely, those ends: that is, with procreation, children, the next generation. In the matter-of-fact phrase of one highly regarded manual of ethnography, "Marriage is a union between a man and a woman such that the children born to the woman are recognized as legitimate offspring of both partners." If, as has been said, children are the ultimate "illegal aliens," then the purpose of marriage is to provide them with the full rights of human citizenship, including public legitimacy, social identity, legal recognition, a lineage, a cultural tradition, and an estate.

When it comes to the nurture and protection of children, moreover, marriage is by far the best arrangement ever devised—which is one reason we find it in all human societies, primitive and modern, ancient and contemporary, Western and non-Western. Cultures that differ on many things all agree that children should not be born outside of marriage, an institution that lays the legal foundation for the family that will be formed by it.

In imposing obligations on parents with regard to children, marriage ensures that every child has a *pater*, the socially recognized father who assumes full responsibility for that child, and not merely a *genitor*, a biological father. It also establishes the cultural context in which children learn to respect the authority of parents. When a child is born to a marriage, mother, father, and all their relatives are now attached to that creature whose well-being has been placed within their care. Later, much later, when the children grow up and the parents grow old, the situation subtly reverses itself; the web of obligation remains constant and unbroken.

III

But I have been speaking too abstractly and, alas, too positively. Can we say of American society at large that in it, for the most part, the web of obligation remains constant and unbroken? Hardly; otherwise, we would not be hearing so much, including from the likes of me, about the crisis of marriage and the family, or about the powerlessness of government alone to affect that crisis.

My argument here is that the family is and always has been the first and most important incubator of those habits of trust, altruism, responsibility, and mutual obligation on which civil society depends— in Michael Novak's words, the first, best, and original department of health, education, and welfare. Any society desirous of preserving itself has, therefore, the strongest possible interest in the well-being of its families, and especially in the safety and protection of its children. That interest, it is fair to say, has been subverted by the steady assault on marriage and family that I have detailed in earlier chapters, a process colluded in by government, furthered by the hedonistic and liberationist march of our culture, and abetted by the erosion of once inviolate boundaries of decorum—whether in the White House or on the movie screen, in our neighborhoods or, sad to say, even in some of our churches.

Shall I recount the damage once more? Since 1960, the divorce rate has more than doubled, out-of-wedlock births have skyrocketed from one in twenty to one in three, the percentage of single-parent families has more than tripled, the number of couples cohabiting has increased more than elevenfold, the fertility rate has decreased by almost half. In record numbers, we have seen fathers deserting their wives and children—and being permitted to do so without reproach or penalty of any kind. We have seen stay-at-home mothers mocked. We have seen the advent of something called the "parenting deficit"—a polite way of saying that many parents are, in effect, absent from their children's lives.

Along with this transformation of reality, we have also seen a dramatic shift in people's *attitudes* toward marriage and the family: toward the expectations that should govern male-female relationships, toward the responsibilities of parenthood, and toward sex itself, which has been untethered from any notion of committed love. Once almost universally regarded as a sacred covenant, marriage and family life now strike many people as provisional undertakings at best. They have been encouraged in this mental direction by feminists, academic analysts with an agenda, and libertines masquerading as liberationists: a de facto coalition of cultural voices arguing that the very institution of the family is inherently oppressive, a reflection of the power preferences of males, or at best an arbitrary construct infinitely adaptable to whatever ends free individuals may wish to devise for it.

Applied to the laws, the morals, and the civic and religious life of our society, these notions and others like them have wrought carnage. Indeed, when we think back on the recent past, does it not begin to seem naive in the extreme that we should ever have expected otherwise? There are traditional moral understandings that may be refined and qualified, but that cannot be flouted with impunity. There is a natural order that we may build on and improve but that we attempt to do away with at peril of the very fabric of our lives, our happiness, our true and solid contentment. Too many of us have attempted to do just that and have reaped a whirlwind.

IV

What, then, should we do? Have we reached the condition, so well described by the Roman historian Livy, where we can neither endure our vices nor face their remedy, unwilling perhaps to go on indefinitely with a society whose families are so fragmented but unable to do what is required to strengthen them? In pointing a way out of our predicament, I wish to offer not so much a detailed blueprint as a few essential guidelines.

The first order of business must be to develop a new and clearer frame of mind. Sadly, there are those who have concluded from surveying the damage that the collapse of the family is indeed irreversible. (I exclude those who have consciously worked for the collapse of the family, and welcome it.) My response is that this need not be so, and that we must not allow it to be so.

Other social problems once thought to be intractable have, after all, yielded to resolute action, and in some cases with stunning swiftness. During the second half of the 1990s, welfare rolls decreased by almost half, and the murder rate dropped to its lowest level since the 1960s. And we have made progress on other "entrenched" social problems as well: racism, poverty, the use of illegal drugs, drunk driving. Even some of the pathologies related to the American family have slowed or diminished in recent years. We are not helpless or without recourse when it comes to repairing damage we have sustained. Our injuries are in most cases self-inflicted; they can be self-corrected. They are the consequences of moral choice; they can be redressed by means of other, better choices.

Second, we need to be realistic. Many of the changes, especially the economic and technological changes, that have affected our families will not be undone. Many, indeed, should not be undone. Over the centuries, as I have chronicled in Chapter Two, quite a few aspects of marriage and family life have changed for the better. To take some obvious examples: Unlike in ages past, the vast majority of us do not practice or believe in arranged marriages, let alone in polygamy, nor do we countenance for a moment the denial of a woman's legal rights in marriage. In deciding to marry, we moderns place the emphasis on voluntary and reciprocal affection, on emotional fulfillment, friendship, and companionship. The last few decades, moreover, have seen other changes in marriage and family life. Many men are more involved in the early raising of their children, and wives in truly bad marriages have more avenues for protecting themselves or, if necessary, for escape.

Surely this is to the good and constitutes authentic progress. If we insist on retaining an image of family life drawn in the exact lineaments of a Major Ballou or a Teddy Rooosevelt, we will certainly fail in our efforts. And yet many Americans who have no desire to regress into a lost past are nevertheless appalled at the social chaos we have created and are eager for what might be called a *restoration,* or what the writer Tom Wolfe has called a "great relearning."

The moment is ripe. The Promethean arrogance of the last

decades, having wrought so much misery, has shown signs of slowly exhausting itself, which means the ground may be readier for fresh starts than it once was even a short while ago. My hope is that many more of us will join in recognizing the opportunity and in building on it.

Third, and in line with what I have just said, we need to disseminate the facts—the truth—about marriage and family life, for facts are our greatest allies. The more we know and can tell about the real-life benefits of marriage and family—and the more we know and can tell about the real-life harm of the effort to undo them—the stronger becomes our case.

Fourth, Americans in positions of leadership need to assert and to argue—publicly, consistently, and compellingly—that their goal is to fortify marriage and the family. This message can come from figures in many different fields: religion, education, entertainment, sports, business, medicine, law, the military, politics. To take an obvious example, President George W. Bush could find few more significant uses of his bully pulpit than in helping to shape public attitudes toward the family for the better.

Fifth, at every level of government we need to implement *policies* that strengthen both marriage and the family. I have already proposed a number of such policies, from reforming no-fault divorce laws to supporting the Defense of Marriage Act to cutting off future welfare benefits to unmarried teen mothers. More can be found in a document titled *The Marriage Movement: A Statement of Principles.** Enacting these reforms would mark a positive advance if only because for far too many years our government and our laws

---

* Coalition for Marriage, Family and Couples Education; Institute for American Values; Religion, Culture, and Family Project, University of Chicago Divinity School, July 2000.

have put themselves on the side of decomposition, not on the side of restoration. But laws also give expression to our moral beliefs. The civil rights legislation of the 1950s and 1960s represented a sterling example of statecraft as soulcraft. It is time we undertook to fight with equal ardor and determination on behalf of our most precious institution.

In the end, however, our ability to reclaim lost ground will depend far less on external rules and regulations, let alone on government, than on the disposition of individual minds and hearts. Our attitudes, our beliefs, and our inner convictions determine what we esteem and what we consider worthy. And these attitudes and convictions, exemplified in our character, in our behavior, and in our teaching, will shape the future.

It has become a cliché to invoke the dizzying pace of change that characterizes today's world. Change is, indeed, undeniable; but amid all this change, some things remain constant. They include, preeminently, what is required of us as good husbands and wives and parents: daily acts of love and devotion, compassion and self-sacrifice, encouragement and generosity.

The blessings that come to us through marriage and parenthood—I speak here of the deepest kind of human fulfillment—are immeasurable and irreplaceable and, as Teddy Roosevelt reminds us, incomparable. We live in an age in which we are continually being torn away from that which is priceless and enduring. This means that ours is the task of reminding ourselves, and each other, not only of what we have lost but of what, when it comes to marriage and the family, is still ours to regain: a little of the calm assurance of a T.R., a little of the luminous clarity of a Sullivan Ballou.

In that spirit, I hope it will not be taken amiss if I conclude with a few home truths about and for marriage in particular—not about its social utility but about its inward meaning. I focus on marriage rather than the family because marriage is a public act, because it properly precedes and is the antecedent condition for the formation of a family, and because it is still, despite everything, a magnet of our hopes and expectations. But I hardly mean to sever it from family, for marriage and parenthood are also, when all is said and done, inextricable.

One of the most public acts connected with marriage is also, paradoxically, one of the most personal and private: the solemn vows exchanged between bride and groom at a wedding ceremony in the presence of friends and family and (to quote the familiar words) in the sight of God. We moderns are rather too quick to dismiss the power of such rituals. But as symbolic acts they express not only moral sentiments but otherwise inexpressible resolves. Often, they help us to define what it means to be fully human, and even to lift us, however briefly, beyond the sphere of the human.

A common occurrence at weddings is that friends and family of the bride and groom find their *own* feelings about marriage reawakened, their own solemn undertakings renewed. Such is the power of ritual. "In sickness and in health," "in sorrow and in joy," "forsaking all others," "till death us do part": Hearing or recalling those deeply resonant phrases, we are reminded that for the vast majority of us, the marriage ceremony is not only a moment of joy but a moment of serious and reverent commitment.

It is possible, of course, for people to carry out commitments in the absence of formal sanctions and elevated language. But the marriage ritual, like the marriage certificate, reinforces these commitments in a wholly unique fashion, casting its aura over every moment of shared significance in the life of a wedded couple—including the moments of trial and exasperation.

The Book of Proverbs speaks of friends sharpening each other "as iron sharpens iron," but this is even truer of marriage. In an apt metaphor, Dr. Timothy J. Keller of New York's Redeemer Presbyterian Church offers the image of a gem tumbler. Like this device, marriage induces what he terms "constructive conflict," steadily knocking off rough edges until a stone emerges that is smoother, more beautiful, more polished, and more perfect than when it went in.

This "tumbling" process is sometimes no picnic. The truth is that marriage can lead to some startling revelations. As premarriage counselors often remind couples, married life brings to the surface your *worst* attributes: irritability and impatience, defensiveness and self-justification, insensitivity and manipulativeness, and, above all, selfishness. Marriage does not create these traits in us; it exposes them.

The point, however, is not simply to learn to recognize faults. A good marriage teaches what it means to forgive, to let go of grievances, to yield when appropriate, to compromise and work together toward a common goal, to put the interests of another above your own. It is because these things do not come naturally that marriage is so good for so many of us, making us in the end more responsible and committed, more self-controlled and compassionate, more purposive and more fulfilled than we would ever have been had we remained single.

Marriage lets us open ourselves *completely* to another human being. For newly married couples, this can be an unnerving experience—and for good reason. There is considerable personal risk involved in so high a degree of openness and vulnerability. That is precisely why it is so important for marriage to be seen both as an enduring and as an exclusive relationship; only the sense of both permanence and exclusivity creates the security that makes such a risk worth taking. And yet, once taken, it can lead to an intimacy that is unparalleled, and whose gifts are unceasing.

For me, though, the real heart of the matter is this: Marriage, a social institution, enshrines such deep truths about the human condition itself as to bespeak a transcendent understanding of the purposes of life on earth. I fully recognize that I cannot "prove" this in the sense that one can prove, say, a scientific proposition or a mathematical equation. But I assert it with confidence, for much of human experience bears witness to its truth.

As I have stated repeatedly in this book, I believe there are certain givens in the human condition. Among them are that we need to love and be loved. We have deep longings for sexual intimacy and emotional attachment. We hope to achieve completeness as human beings, to satisfy the yearnings of our souls. And we long for a safe haven in this world, a home, and children to have, to love, to nurture.

Some of these desires can be met by close friends and kin. But preeminently it is marriage—the voluntary, lifelong, exclusive commitment to a person of the opposite sex—that comes closest to satisfying our deepest longings. Along with parenthood, having your heart braided to another human being is life's most vivifying experience. "What greater thing is there for two human souls," asked George Eliot, "than to feel that they are joined for life—to strengthen each other in all labor, to rest on each other in all sorrow, to minister to each other in all pain, to be one with each other in silent, unspeakable memories at the moment of the last parting?"

Marital love rooted in unconditional commitment is safer, more enduring, and more empowering than any sentiment yet discovered or any human arrangement yet invented. That is because marriage rests on the basic complementarity of man and woman, the complementarity that drives two independent people to become, in the biblical phrase, "one flesh." And this complementarity is itself based on fundamental differences between men and women that are physical and emotional, psychological and sexual. Indeed, it is these very differences—these complementary differences—that help men and women achieve, in marriage, unity and interdependence, completeness and fulfillment.

One obvious feature of male-female complementarity is the sexual. In conjugal sex, men and women give to each other fully, completely, exclusively. In this, too, I would argue, there is an exalted aspect. True sexual love is not about treating the other person as an object of desire. It is, rather, about "self-giving," an act that in deep and even paradoxical ways confers dignity and worth upon—I would say giver and receiver alike, except that both receive in giving, and both give in receiving. Sexual love of this kind is a profoundly *moral* act, and when and if it leads to that utterly commonplace occurrence of a man and woman creating a new life, it is also an utterly miraculous one.

In healthy marriages, men and women seek to perfect themselves for the sake of the other. Day in and day out, they offer and draw moral strength, sharing compassion, courage, honesty, self-discipline, and a host of other virtues. The whole of the union becomes stronger than the sum of the parts. If there is an element of self-sacrifice in this enterprise—and there assuredly is—that, too, like sex, is part of the mystery of this divine-human institution.

V

Researchers tell us that married life offers us many things: more financial security, better sex, better health, longer and better days on earth. I have gone over these matters, and in and of themselves they certainly make marriage worth defending. But they are not, in the end, what marriage is about. At its core marriage is what it has always been: "an honorable estate, instituted of God." It offers husbands and wives what Wordsworth called intimations of immortality. At its finest, I would go so far as to say marital love is a reflection of divine love, resplendent and sublime.

In all Christian traditions, one of the chief purposes of marriage is sanctification; in Catholicism, marriage is explicitly designated as a sacrament. The Book of Common Prayer captures this conception in the phrase I just quoted: "an honorable estate, instituted of God." In Jewish tradition, similarly, betrothal itself carries the name of "sanctification"; at a Jewish wedding ceremony, in placing a ring on his bride's finger, the groom recites a formula beginning "Be thou *consecrated* unto me." These common understandings are very ancient and very basic.

What raises marital love to the level of sanctity, what makes it a reflection of divine love, is the act of creation. For marriage is the prelude to family, and marriage and parenthood, as I have said, are inextricable. Yes, some people marry and consciously decide not to have children; yes, some people have children without benefit of marriage. But I would maintain, with respect, that in both cases they have missed out on what has ever been for most human beings the central experience and the twinned, incommunicable core of life itself. Indeed, the detachment of human coupling from the institutions of marriage and the family is itself, I would argue, a sign of our larger detachment from the springs of our existence on earth.

Earlier I wrote that we must not invest hopes in our marriages or in our families that can never be realized. The point bears repeating. But neither should we invest less hope than is warranted. We need to see marriage and family both realistically and in terms of their highest purposes. We need to recognize that with all their attendant duties and commitments and responsibilities, their common touchstone is love, and in them we need to repose both our faith and our determination to succeed.

For the blessings of marriage and family life are indeed recoverable. If we do our part, there is reason to hope that those blessings may yet again be ours—ours to have, ours to hold, ours to bequeath to our children.

Index

Printed in the United States
by Baker & Taylor Publisher Services